LAW AND OBEDIENCE:
THE ARGUMENTS OF PLATO'S *CRITO*

Law and Obedience:
The Arguments of
Plato's *Crito*

A. D. WOOZLEY

The University of North Carolina Press
Chapel Hill

First published in 1979 by
Gerald Duckworth & Company Limited
The Old Piano Factory
43 Gloucester Crescent, London NW1

ISBN 0–8078–1366–4

Library of Congress Catalog Card Number 79–456

Library of Congress Cataloging in Publication Data

Woozley, Anthony Douglas.
  Law and obedience.
  Includes index.
    1. Plato. Crito. 2. Law—Philosophy.
  3. Obedience. 4. Socrates. I. Title.
  B368.W66 1979   172'.1   79–456

  ISBN 0–8078–1366–4

Printed in Great Britain by
Latimer Trend & Company Ltd Plymouth

Contents

To C.D.

Preface

This book, the aim of which is explained in the introductory chapter, is written in the belief that the arguments given in the *Crito* why it is wrong to break the law are interestingly bad rather than uninterestingly good. I have allowed myself to pursue ideas suggested by repeated readings of the dialogue, and to discuss questions which never entered Socrates' head; at the same time I have tried to avoid the sin of misattribution. I have been helped by comments from many people, and especially by the detailed criticisms which I have received from my colleagues Daniel Devereux and Cora Diamond, the latter of whom also relieved me of the chore of compiling the index. I am greatly indebted to Russell Dancy, who vetted my translation of the *Crito* and saved me from several disasters. My thanks go too to a pair of patient and persevering typists, Eusebia Shifflett and John Knight.

Part of Chapter Three, in an earlier version, appeared as an article in the 1976 issue of *Paideia*, and I acknowledge the editor's permission to reproduce it.

Finally, I owe a debt of gratitude to the University of Virginia for assigning me to wholetime research duties for part of 1977, thereby enabling me to finish the book.

A.D.W.

CHAPTER ONE

Introductory

The *Crito* is, by general consensus, one of the earliest of Plato's dialogues; and it is also one of the shortest. In view of the setting and of the topics of discussion, it is extremely difficult not to believe that it is offered as a substantially accurate account of Socrates' conduct at the time, and of his views which determined that conduct. In one important respect it is not a typically Socratic dialogue; but, just in that respect, it brings out the seriousness of Socrates' commitment to his moral views.

Dramatically, it is the third of a group of four works covering the period of the trial and death of Socrates in 399 B.C. The *Euthyphro* opens with Socrates giving the news that he is about to be prosecuted on the two charges of religious heresy and of corrupting the minds of the young; but the subject is not mentioned again in the brief philosophical duologue which follows between Socrates and Euthyphro. The *Apology*, the only one of Plato's works (apart from the *Letters*) not written in dialogue form presents, or purports to present, the three speeches made by Socrates at his trial: his unsuccessful defence to the charges, his unsuccessful proposal for the sentence, and his final address to the court. The *Crito*, again a duologue, this time between Socrates and Crito, an elderly and wealthy friend, portrays their conversation in Socrates' gaol cell several weeks later, and two days before the death penalty which the court had imposed was due to be carried out. The conversation consists wholly of Crito urging Socrates to allow his friends to arrange an eleventh-hour escape from prison, and of Socrates giving reasons why, even though the trial had been a travesty of justice, it would be wrong for him to agree. Finally, the *Phaedo* recounts a philosophical conversation between Socrates and a number of his friends on the actual day set for the execution of the sentence, and ends with a description of Socrates drinking the hemlock and dying.

The actual order of composition of the four works is probably not quite the same as their dramatic order: the *Euthyphro*, in which, as already indicated, the charges against Socrates are just mentioned as a lead-in to the philosophical topic of the dialogue, was almost certainly written somewhat later than the *Apology* and the *Crito*. And, although the interval between the composition of the *Apology* and that of the *Crito* is likely to have been very short, the *Phaedo* appears to have been written considerably later. In every way it is a much more complicated composition than its predecessors. Structurally, it is a dialogue within a dialogue: Phaedo gives to a friend his own eyewitness account of Socrates' last day alive, and how he spent it discussing with those present the question of the immortality of the soul, and other philosophical problems arising from that. Plato may have employed the device of representing the main dialogue as reported later by one of the participants in it, in order to emphasise the point, which he does once mention (59b10), that he himself was not present, and therefore could not in his own person report Socrates' final conversation. Dramatically, the *Phaedo* is more sophisticated, in that there are more parties to the conversation than in the common pattern of the early dialogues: Socrates and one other person (as in both the *Euthyphro* and the *Crito*). And philosophically it is enormously richer and more complex, ideas beginning to emerge in it which are more associated with Plato himself than with Socrates.

As Socrates himself wrote nothing, and as we are dependent for our knowledge of his way of philosophising and of his philosophical views almost entirely on the representation of them in Plato's dialogues, the question how accurately particular dialogues present him, or even are intended to present him, can be difficult. But the *Apology* and the *Crito* are special cases, their circumstances marking them off from other works by Plato. Both were probably written very shortly after Socrates' death. As Socrates' trial had been held in public, and the arguments which he used in his defence would be well known to many in Athens, Plato, even if he had wanted to, could hardly have afforded substantially to misreport them in the *Apology*. And, as the *Crito* is something of a devoted pupil's obituary tribute to his master, we should need overwhelmingly good reasons for believing that that too is not substantially faithful. (An attempt has been made by Gilbert Ryle to establish that the two works are considerably later in composition, and that they are Plato's defence of himself, not his account of Socrates' defence of *himself*.[1] But Ryle's late dating of the *Apology* and the *Crito* has nothing beyond its own ingenuity to recommend it. The latest stylistic analysis by L. Brandwood, places them firmly in the earliest group of Platonic dialogues.)[2]

It strains credulity to ask us to believe that in the *Crito*, of all dialogues, Plato would have portrayed Socrates as holding views which he did not hold, still less that, if it had not been true, he would have put into Socrates' mouth a speech insisting that the views which he is now expressing are not those of a just-before-death conversion, but ones which he has held all along (49a–b). But some have thought that it is impossible that both works should be giving an accurate account of Socrates' views on the individual's duty of obedience to law, on the ground that his position in the one flatly contradicts his position in the other. Specifically, the objection is that, as in the *Apology* he expresses his determination to defy a court order prohibiting him from engaging in further public philosophising (29c–d), and as in the *Crito* he declares that the individual must obey the court, no matter what (50b–c), at least one of the accounts cannot be accurately reporting Socrates; and some further explanation is required why Plato represented him as taking two such violently contrary stands, one at his trial and the other barely four weeks afterwards. This will be discussed in more detail later.

The respect in which the *Crito* does not conform to the type of the early, so-called Socratic, dialogues is interesting. The general pattern of an early dialogue is for Socrates to engage the other party (sometimes one person, sometimes more) in the search for the definition of a virtue, e.g. piety (*Euthyphro*), temperance (*Charmides*), courage (*Laches*), justice (*Republic*, Bk I). He usually gets a confident answer, which by asking awkward questions and posing awkward counterexamples he

[1] Gilbert Ryle, *Plato's Progress* (Cambridge: Cambridge University Press, 1966), ch. v.
[2] v. J. B. Skemp, *Plato* (*Greece and Rome*, New Surveys in the Classics, no. 10. Oxford: Clarendon Press, 1976), p. 14, and n. 12.

deflates. The process will be repeated several times, with definitions being suggested, all of them meeting the same fate, punctured by Socrates. The net result is that, after an exercise in analytical philosophy, the other party is shown (and may admit that he has been shown) not to have known what he thought he did; and the discussion ends negatively, with no direct conclusions established beyond that the answers so far offered have been wrong. The *Euthyphro* is an excellent example, where Euthyphro, after he has suggested (sometimes led on by Socrates) five different definitions of piety and has seen each of them shot down in turn, calls off the conversation by saying that he has a pressing engagement elsewhere. If that was, as it seems to have been, Socrates' usual practice, and if he particularly attracted the young both to participate with him and to observe him discountenancing their elders by persistently showing up the weaknesses and fallacies in their assumptions and arguments, it is hardly surprising that he acquired the reputation of ruining the young by encouraging them to question everything. An iconoclast who claims to be superior to others in just one respect, viz. that he knows (while they do not) how much he does not know is unlikely to commend himself to an intolerant society.

The *Crito*, however, is not another exhibition of Socratic analysis; it is not a search for a philosophically satisfactory account of a moral concept. The questions asked are substantive moral questions, before which philosophers have a way of pulling up short, as though the purity of moral principles and of forms of moral argument make it improper for them to pronounce moral views on actual, or even imaginary, individual cases. The question in the *Crito* is whether it would be wrong for Socrates to take advantage of the escape from gaol which his friends are offering him. After Crito has briefly recited what seem to him good reasons why Socrates *ought* to allow the escape to be effected, Socrates takes over and for the rest of the dialogue goes through the reasons why it would be wrong for him to agree. That is, we get from him not only his rebuttal of the other person's views (as in the other dialogues), but also a fairly detailed statement of his own. Instead of Socrates asking the questions we have Socrates giving the answers (in the words of the personified laws of Athens), the principal answer being that on his duty to obey the law, and on the reasons why it is his duty. As the three distinct reasons which Socrates offers why he ought, and therefore why anybody ought whose circumstances are not significantly different, to obey the law are reasons which are still among the first to be offered why we ought to obey the law, the *Crito* is much more than a suitably short and a suitably clear Platonic dialogue for the student to cut his philosophical teeth on. The issues which it raises about what it is to live in society subject to law are immense; and, because pursuit of them will take us far away from the text of the dialogue, this book is not to be thought of as a commentary in the usual sense. On the other hand, the text, both of the *Crito* and of those parts of the *Apology* which are relevant, will have to be examined with some care and in detail. It is only by glossing over the detail that it is possible, as is sometimes done, to portray Socrates as unequivocally holding that a man should always obey the law. It is less troublesome not to attend to the detail, because then one can present his position as being clearer and more univocal than it was. But inaccuracy is too high a price to pay for the elegance of simplicity; and in the end it may turn out that, if we assume Plato's account to be faithful, Socrates had not entirely cleared up his own mind on questions which are easy only at the superficial level at which most politicians operate.

To some readers it may appear from time to time that I talk about Socrates, and attribute views to him, when the question is whether they should rather be attributed to Plato. I do throughout the book treat the 'Socrates' of the *Crito* as a real person, and not as a character in a play by Plato, partly because I believe that the dialogue, like the *Apology*, was intended to be a substantially faithful representation of the actual Socrates, but even more because the purposes of the book do not demand that the authorship of this view or that, even if it could, should be exactly established. The views as presented, and the reasons advanced for them, are what here matter; it is more important that they be correctly interpreted and fairly assessed than that they be properly attributed to 'Socrates' rather than to Socrates, or *vice versa*.

CHAPTER TWO

Socrates' Rebuttal of Crito's Arguments for Escape

The problem of the *Crito* is a problem of conduct, and an actual, not an imaginary, problem: should Socrates give or refuse his consent to a plan by his friends to rescue him from gaol before his death sentence can be carried out? It is a problem for the discussion of which the duologue form is admirably suited, because all the arguments on the one side can be presented by Crito, and all the objections to them and all the arguments on the other side can be presented by Socrates. Philosophically, it would have been a fuller discussion if Crito had been up to propounding the objections to Socrates' own arguments, but he was not; and no doubt the actual Socrates in no small degree owed his eminence and reputation, and ironically his eventual fate, to his being quicker on his feet than those with whom he argued. The dramatic urgency of the problem is highlighted by the opening lines, which disclose that Crito has arrived at the gaol much earlier in the day than usual, indeed some time before dawn, because he bears the news that Socrates' execution is likely to be fixed for the following day (43d); and by his stressing that Socrates must make up his mind at once, because the last opportunity for carrying out the escape will be that night (46a). Socrates thereupon, as if to provide Dr Johnson with an illustration of his opinion that the prospect of execution concentrates a man's mind wonderfully, sets to to pick Crito's case to pieces.

Crito advances four reasons why Socrates should give his consent to the planned escape, all of them pointing out what will happen, if he does not consent:

1. He will be robbing Crito of a friend such as he will never find again (44b). Nothing is made of this reason. It is simply

mentioned, in specification of one half of the double disaster which Socrates' death will be for Crito, and as a preface to the second reason ('apart from the fact of my being deprived of a friend . . .'). And Socrates does not bother to answer it. It is natural to ask why Plato, in composing the dialogue, had Crito raise the point and Socrates ignore it; the most natural answer seems to be that it is his way of expressing to the reader the kind of muddleheadedness in argument which he wishes Crito to represent. It is not even clear that it is being offered as a moral reason, rather than a plea from one person to another not to treat him in a certain way. Pleas, for example, of the about-to-be-abandoned lover, 'Don't leave me', 'Don't do that to me', are not obviously moral pleas, and at their lowest can be simply self-pitying. But such a plea *can* convey a genuine moral claim; it may be true, in given circumstances, that one person ought, out of pity, to do what another person is pleading with him ('for my sake') to do. A similar consideration applies to Crito's second reason, and much more clearly, because he gives that reason in far more detail; and indeed it is the only one which Socrates seems to think worth serious refutation. As will be shown, the general point which Crito makes there is entirely valid; how strictly it applies to the particular case of himself, and whether his claiming that it does is to his credit, are other questions. Socrates does not emerge from that exchange too well: he dismisses cavalierly the point which Crito had made, and then gets him to agree with an argument which he propounds as being damaging to Crito's thesis, but which is strictly at cross-purposes with it.

2. Crito's second reason is summarily that, if Socrates goes to his death, then Crito himself will acquire the dishonourable reputation among the many who do not know him of being a man who could have saved Socrates' life but failed to do so because he was not willing to spend the money which the scheme would cost. Who was going to believe that it was the other way round, that he was eager to do it, and that it was Socrates himself who refused (44b–c)? After a brief rejoinder by Socrates and Crito's reply to that, the latter then cites his third and fourth reasons. Of these, Socrates ignores one and cursorily dismisses the other, then reverting to the issue which he thinks to have been raised by Crito's second reason. The important

question is not whether public opinion thinks it would be right for Socrates to be saved by an escape plan, or wrong for Crito and Socrates' other friends not to rescue him, but whether an escape really would be right (48c–d).

Discussion of Crito's second reason will be taken up below, after first completing his list by giving his last two reasons. Whether or not he regarded (2) as being a moral reason (a question to be returned to shortly), he certainly so regarded (3) and (4), which he introduces by saying that it would not be morally right (δίκαιον) for Socrates to pursue his present course (45c).

3. By throwing away his life, when he could be saved, Socrates is striving for the very outcome for which his enemies would have striven, and for which those who wanted to ruin him did strive (45c). As it stands, that argument hardly merits a reply; and it gets none from Socrates. Crito's thought probably is that it would be irrational for Socrates to do his enemies' job for them, especially when the job was that of bringing about his own death. And perhaps again Plato is using Crito to present a case that misses the point: Crito does not understand that Socrates' real enemies are not the men who are trying to have him killed, but his own desires which urge him to a solution other than death; so, he will not be cooperating with his enemies if he goes to his death, but he will be if he allows himself to be rescued. Viewed as a moral argument Crito's case has a certain plausibility about it, for it rests on a general proposition that, if a certain end would be bad if attained by one person (in this case, any member of the class of Socrates' enemies), then it would be bad if attained by another (in this case, Socrates himself). But a universalisability proposition as crude as that cannot be defended. Starting from the premise that it was wrong for Socrates' enemies to try to bring about his death we cannot infer that it must be wrong for Socrates to bring about his death, unless we know that there are no relevant differences in the circumstances; the mere fact that what each is trying to achieve is the same is not enough to make it wrong in one case if wrong in the other. And an obvious difference is that, as Socrates himself later emphasises, he is bringing about his own death in obedience to the order of a court; if there are overwhelming reasons (and he is going to argue that there are)

why the sentence of a court, whatever it is, should be upheld, then he is morally bound to accept death in obedience to the law (50b–c). And in the *Phaedo* Plato represents him as arguing that, although suicide is morally wrong, yet in his own case drinking the hemlock will, strictly speaking, not be suicide, because he will be acting as the agent of a higher authority (62c). Socrates' exact position on the duty of a man under orders to obey them is not entirely clear, and will be returned to later.

4. By allowing the death sentence to be carried out Socrates will be failing his sons; instead of bringing them up and educating them himself he will be abandoning them to whatever may befall them as orphans. Either a man should not have children at all; or, if he does, then he ought to go right through with their upbringing and education (45c–d). The only direct response which Socrates makes to this claim may seem curiously callous. Having given in some detail his rejection of Crito's second reason, he then lumps it together with this last one and says 'the considerations which you raise about spending money, and one's reputation, and bringing up children are just the notions of those many people who, without any understanding, would lightly kill a man, and bring him back to life again, if they were able to' (48c). The idea that children have any rights to certain treatment by their parents is a popular but baseless cliché. Socrates' apparent hardheartedness may seem to fit an analogy which he later uses when arguing for his duty to obey the law (50d–51c); he might there again be read as maintaining that, while parents have absolute rights to treat their children as they see fit, children have no corresponding rights against their parents. But, in fact, he is not there making such a sweeping, indeed staggering, claim. There are various limitations put on it, the relevant one being that a father's rights against his children stem from what he has done for them by rearing and educating them. Socrates is not there denying that fathers have a duty to provide for their children's upbringing and education (indeed he explicitly refers to the laws of Athens requiring it); but, by the discharge of that duty a father acquires rights in relation to his children, which they do not acquire in relation to him. That is not quite the same as the view expressed by Aristotle, that a child below a certain age and before he has

set out on a life of his own is a part of his father, so that the question of a child's rights, or of a violation of them, could not arise (*NE* 1134b). Strictly, a man could not be unjust to what belonged to him—either to what he owned (such as his slaves) or to what was part of him (such as his children); it is impossible for a man to be unjust to himself. At the back of Aristotle's argument is the thesis that a necessary condition of being treated unjustly (which would imply having rights) is being an individual person; and for being that neither a slave, nor a child below a certain age (not specified), qualifies. Socrates, although he does bracket slaves and offspring together (50e), does not make a child's nonpossession of rights against his father turn on his being part of the father, and does not suggest that, after reaching a certain age, he may acquire them or lose certain duties. Indeed that, as will be shown later, is going to turn out to be a principal weakness of his attempt to represent the citizen's relation to the law as the relation of child to father.

But, if Socrates insists (50d) that a father has a duty, properly backed by law, to educate his children, why does he so lightly shrug off, under the heading of popular and ignorant opinion, Crito's suggestion that he himself is about to neglect that very duty (48c)? *Prima facie*, there is an inconsistency which needs explaining or explaining away. It could be explained away, if what Socrates was dismissing as popular nonsense were, not the view that a father has a duty to get his children educated, but the factual premise in Crito's argument, viz. that children left orphans are usually neglected. Unfortunately, he never does that. What he does do is to say, or rather to represent the personified laws of Athens as saying, that his children will be as well off if he dies as if he lives. For, if he lived, he would have to escape into exile; if his children accompanied him, they would suffer the disadvantages of being brought up as foreigners; if instead they remained behind in Athens, they would be looked after by his friends. How could he believe that his friends would look after them in that event, but not in the event that he died (54a)? A cogent argument why Socrates should not worry about his children's fate, but not a refutation of Crito's point that orphans are usually neglected. That the generalisation would not apply in Socrates' case, because he could count on his friends to look after his children, and that consequently he would not be failing in his paternal duty by choosing to leave them orphans do nothing to show the generalisation to be false, or to be a public fixed idea based on ignorance. And, if Socrates believed, as it is implied in 54a that he did, that the generalisation would not apply in his case, then he should have objected, not that it should be disregarded as a popular but ignorant belief, but that it should be disregarded as irrelevant to his case. It is hard to avoid the conclusion that what Socrates was belittling was not a supposedly factual proposition about what usually happens to children left orphaned, but the supposed importance of a father's duty to rear and educate his children. Whether he thought the popular view exaggerated what a father owed his children, or whether he thought one should not make too much of it because, if the father was not there to see to their education, somebody else would, we cannot tell; at least he seems to have thought that one should not make too much of it. And this would harmonise with the final admonition which he imagines the laws giving him: 'but, Socrates, in obedience to us who reared you do not make either children or life or anything else to be of more account than what is right' (54b). It fits too with the final scene of the *Phaedo*, where Plato represents Crito as asking Socrates if he has any instructions for himself or for the others present about his children, and Socrates as replying that he has none (115b). It is not exactly the view that children are expendable, but it shows a certain detachment.

Let us now return to Crito's second reason why Socrates should allow himself to be rescued by an escape plan: that, if he does not, Crito and his other friends (45b) will acquire the public reputation of being men who, when they easily could have saved Socrates' life, failed to through miserliness (44c) or through lack of courage (45e). This is the one reason which Crito most emphasises of the four, it is the only one which Socrates believes to call for detailed refutation, and it is the one which leads directly into the main theme of the dialogue, viz. why and under what conditions it is wrong to disobey the law.

First, what *sort* of a reason is Crito advancing? On one reading, it would be purely self-regarding: Crito is concerned with his own public image, which will look bad if he does not rescue Socrates; and he is saying to Socrates, in effect, 'Don't

think of yourself, think of me.' In the light of Crito's general
character as it appears in the dialogue and in the *Phaedo* this
would be a most implausible reading, which we should be
justified in adopting only in desperation, if we were unable to
find any other; and, fortunately, that is not the case. There has
been some hesitation to accept his reason as a proffered moral
reason, as a reason why Socrates morally ought to agree to the
escape, because it appears little to Crito's credit that he should
at a time like that call attention to the damage which his public
reputation will suffer. How could Crito believe and maintain
that the rights and wrongs of what for Socrates was literally a
life-and-death matter turned on the consideration of what
people would afterwards think of Crito himself? Now, this
objection to reading Crito's reason as a moral reason is invalid,
and fails to keep distinct the speaker-neutrality of a moral
reason (or of reasons in general) from the question of the propriety or impropriety of a particular person advancing it. If
there is a good reason why a man should in a certain situation
act in a certain way, then it is a good reason regardless of who
enunciates it, even of whether it is enunciated at all. We may
have prejudices against the reasons which a man offers in
justification of his conduct, when we believe, and perhaps
correctly believe, that those were not his reasons for engaging
in that conduct, but we need to be honest and acknowledge
them as prejudices. Few of President Nixon's critics believed
that the reasons which he gave for refusing to release to the
Special Prosecutor and to the House Judiciary Committee recorded tapes and other documents were the reasons why in fact
he was refusing. But that did not automatically make the
reasons which he gave into bad reasons. If the argument that
the separation of powers confers on an incumbent President
absolute rights of confidentiality is a good argument (I am not
saying that it is), then it is a good argument in anybody's
mouth, including the mouth of a President whose personal
interest requires that it be believed to be a good argument,
whether or not it actually is. If it is a good moral reason why A
should not act in a certain way that B will suffer if he does, then
it is a good reason, whoever utters it. If it appears indelicate,
insensitive or indecent of B himself to call A's attention to the
goodness of the reason, or to use it as an inducement to A not

to act in the way in question, that may tell us something about the character or personality of B, but it does nothing to weaken his moral claim that A ought not to act in that way, because B will suffer if he does. If that Crito and others would suffer an undeserved reputation in the event of Socrates' death was a good moral reason in favour of Socrates' agreeing to the escape plan, then it was no less good because it was Crito himself who advanced it.

But was Crito advancing it as a moral reason? And, even if he was not, is it a moral reason, is the fact (when it is one) that something is publicly believed to be the case, even though the belief may be ignorant and actually false, relevant to the question what it would be right for a man to do in a situation which contains that public belief as one of its elements? Socrates unhesitatingly answered no to the second question, but in doing so either missed or ignored the thrust of the Crito argument. The first question, viz. whether Crito advanced it as a moral reason, is not easy to answer definitively. He nowhere makes it clear that it was a moral reason; but he does say that he and his friends will have acted rightly in running whatever personal risks would be involved in rescuing Socrates (45a). When he introduces his third and fourth reasons by saying, 'But further, Socrates, you do not seem to me to be doing at all what is right in . . .' (45c), he might be introducing the two further reasons as moral reasons in contrast with the two earlier ones which were not, or he might be adding them as further moral reasons; from the text there is no way of telling. He does say that the reputation he will get from being thought to have let Socrates down would be a *dishonourable* one (44c); and he summarises his attitude by saying that he is *ashamed* ('both on your account and on ours your friends') that the whole affair seems to have been handled with a lack of courage by all of them, Socrates included; it is going to be a *shameful* outcome both for Socrates and for his friends (45e–46a). That at least suggests that he believed that what people would think of him if Socrates were to die was a good reason why it would be wrong for Socrates to allow himself to die.

Although Socrates treats the argument with contempt, it is not clear that he should. According to him one should ignore the opinion of the many, and attend only to the opinion of the most reasonable men (44c). And to Crito's objection that one should indeed not ignore the opinion of the many because, as illustrated by Socrates' own predicament, they are capable of doing great harm if one gets a bad reputation with them, he replies that it would be splendid if they were capable of doing great harm, for then they would be equally capable of doing great good. But, as things are, they can do neither; for they cannot make a man either sensible or foolish (44c–d). That is not Socrates at his best. Apart from the *non sequitur* involved in the claim that, if the public were capable of doing great harm, it would also be capable of doing great good (it is the same illegitimate use of the argument from capacity for opposites as is employed to silence Polemarchus in *Republic* I), he misses (or fails to address himself to) the point. His remark that the many cannot make a man either wise or foolish is appropriate to his favourite thesis that the greatest good for man is wisdom, and the greatest evil folly. But Crito, in suggesting that the many can do a man the greatest harm, is not thinking of *that* kind of harm at all. What he had in mind was the injury which a man could suffer from gaining a certain public reputation; and his claim was that the fact that the public holds a certain opinion on a given issue can be more important than the question whether that opinion is correct or incorrect. If Socrates was wanting to suggest that what Crito thought of as harm was not really harm at all, and that it does not matter what people do to you, as long as they do not make you foolish (which fortunately the many are incapable of doing), he owed Crito rather more than a one-line assertion of it. He could agree with Crito that the fact of public opinion being incorrect (if it was) would be irrelevant, although his reasons for agreeing would be opposed to Crito's—the latter holding that public opinion, whatever its quality, can harm a man, Socrates holding that public opinion, whatever its quality, cannot. When Crito reverts to the theme (45e–46a), with the observation about being ashamed to be thought cowardly (which he could be thought even if he had not been cowardly), Socrates takes him to be maintaining that in deciding what it would be right or wrong to do a man should be influenced by what popular morality declares it would be right or wrong to do. But it is not clear that that is Crito's position.

In his basic claim Crito was surely right: not that the fact of public opinion must always, or even often, outweigh its quality, but that sometimes it does. Sometimes it is one of the factors which ought to play a role, perhaps a major, even an overwhelming, role in an agent's decision what he ought to do. An excellent, unhappy example was provided in the U.S.A. during the long drawn out, relentless build-up of public suspicion that President Nixon was himself closely implicated in the sorry abuse of constitutional power disclosed by the Watergate affair. Despite his stonewalling, his repeated denials that he had been involved, and his vehement protestations of innocence, fewer and fewer Americans believed him. Eventually a point was reached when some of his staunchest supporters, such as Senator James Buckley and newspaper columnist Joseph Alsop, while still proclaiming their conviction that he was not guilty of the charges being publicly levelled against him, yet declared that he ought to resign from the Presidency, because, whether unfairly or not, he no longer enjoyed the credibility and trust which a President must have. Here were two prominent conservatives, and supporters of Mr Nixon, publicly declaring that the damage which was being done by his public reputation was a more important factor than that the reputation was incorrect. Their judgment, which was widely shared, might have been erroneous, but, even if it was, it was a judgment of a kind that *could* be sound. And the principle behind it was the same as Crito's—that the consequences of not taking into account the fact that a belief is widely held may be more serious in the circumstances of the case than the fact that the belief is ill-informed or even false. This is not the doctrine that public opinion must be pandered to, it is the doctrine that sometimes it is wrong to ignore it. Socrates' rejoinder that public opinion should be ignored because it is fickle *is* relevant to that doctrine, but will not apply in cases where public opinion does not chop and change; there was no seesawing, for example, in the public rating of Nixon's truthfulness during 1973–4.

The weakness of Crito's argument lay in its empirical aspect, its supposed applicability to his own case. Socrates was hardly a popular hero, for whose release or rescue there would be public clamour; indeed Crito himself insisted that it was public clamour that had landed Socrates where he was. It is difficult to believe that in such a context Socrates' friends would have been much accused of stinginess or cowardice because they had not snatched him out of gaol.

There is a line of argument, already mentioned, which Socrates might have used against Crito, designed, not to show that as a matter of fact his reputation would not suffer, but to show that it would not be an evil for him even if it did. And some have maintained that Socrates was relying on it, and therefore was not missing Crito's point.[1] This is the argument that if a man is a good man no evil can befall him either in life or in death; consequently, Crito as a good man will not suffer evil from being popularly maligned.

The trouble with that answer is that the principle on which it depends (that no evil can befall a good man), although it appears in the *Apology* (41d), is not mentioned in the *Crito*. What Socrates uses there is the different principle that wrongdoing is an evil for the wrongdoer (49b), which leads him into the argument that one should never, in whatever circumstances, treat people badly. And, if Crito had turned that argument against him by claiming that Socrates was treating him badly by acting in a way that would subject him to popular contempt, Socrates would have had to revert to the empirical objection— that Crito's good name would not in fact suffer from Socrates' death.

The *Apology* principle (if a man is good no evil can befall him) and the *Crito* principle (doing what is wrong is an evil for the wrongdoer) are formally different principles, such that neither formally entails the other. But we must allow that, if they are filled out in the way that Socrates would have filled them out, it can be seen how closely related they are to each other. When Socrates says that the populace are incapable of doing enormous evil to a man, for they are incapable of making him foolish (44d), he is clearly asserting a causal connexion, or identity, between making a man foolish and doing evil to him. The good man cannot have evil befall him because he knows what a terrible thing it is to do wrong, and, because he knows that, he cannot want to do it. If the only way that evil can

[1] Jeffrie G. Murphy, 'The Socratic theory of legal fidelity', in Philip P. Wiener and John Fisher (eds), *Violence and Aggression in the History of Ideas* (New Brunswick, N.J.: Rutgers University Press, 1974), pp. 15–33.

befall him is through his own wrongdoing, and if because of his knowledge of wrong he cannot want to do it, he cannot do the one thing through which evil can befall him.

It is necessary to keep distinct from each other arguments against Crito's *conclusion* (Socrates ought to agree to the escape) from arguments against Crito's *reasons for* his conclusion. So far Socrates has not reached the stage of producing arguments against the conclusion, although he is now on the threshold of them. What he has done is to maintain that, whatever the status of Crito's conclusion, his reasons for it, even his second reason, are not good reasons.

By misunderstanding or misrepresenting Crito's argument Socrates is able to introduce his own and lead into the central topic of the dialogue. Taking Crito to have said that in deciding what he ought to do a man should consult public opinion on what he ought to do (which is not at all what Crito had originally said), Socrates properly replies that some opinions are better than others (46d), and that he is not prepared to abandon his lifelong principle of accepting only that advice from his friends which on reflection appears best in terms of reason (46b); getting good moral advice is a matter, not of counting heads, but of consulting the most reasonable heads (47a). Here Socrates introduces one of his favourite analogies, the physical condition of the human body: if somebody seriously wants to train himself into good condition, does he not listen to advice on diet and exercise, and to the criticisms and encouragements, of the man who knows, i.e., the doctor or trainer (47b)? And life is not worth living if the body, which is improved by a healthy regime but corrupted by a sick one, is ruined. *A fortiori*, when what is at stake is the health of that in a man which is improved by upright conduct and corrupted by what is wrong, and which is far more valuable to us and important to our life than the condition of the body, it is even more essential to attend only to what the man who knows about right and wrong will say about us (47d–48a). So, Crito had been wrong in maintaining that they ought to pay attention to what public opinion thinks 'about what is right and honourable and good, and their opposites' (48a).

Finally, to the possible objection that one should regard public opinion, because it is able to put us to death, Socrates replies that what matters most is, not living, but living a good life (48b). What has to be faced then, without dragging in any irrelevant considerations about cost, or about what people will think or about the upbringing of one's children, is the question whether it would be just or whether it would be unjust for Socrates to attempt to get away from gaol unless he is officially released; if it appears that it would be unjust, then neither the prospect of death if he remains, nor that of suffering anything else is to count against doing what would be unjust (48c–d).

At this point it is necessary to interject a remark about translation. The verb ἀδικεῖν, together with the adjective ἄδικος, the adverb ἀδίκως, the noun ἀδικία, and the corresponding positives (δίκαια πράττειν, δίκαιος, δικαίως, δικαιοσύνη) always have in Plato a moral sense, and all have a general, and also a specific, sense; one has to judge from the context which is being used. In the general sense the verbs mean 'to do what is wrong/ right', the adjectives 'wrong/right', the adverbs 'wrongly/ rightly', the nouns 'wrongness/rightness'. The specific sense is 'to do what is unjust/just', and similarly for the other parts of speech. Consequently, it is possible for a translator slightly, or even seriously, to mislead a Greekless reader who has no way of exercising his own judgment. For example, despite the tradition of translations, the *Republic* is far more concerned with the right and the good than it is with, more narrowly, the just. In the first six pages of the *Crito* it has not mattered to an understanding or an assessment of Socrates' argument against Crito whether the words were being used in the general or in the specific sense. But from 48c on it does matter. The specific sense is being used, and should be conveyed, as unfortunately often it is not, in English translations. The point about the specific use is that for a man to act unjustly there must be someone else whom he is treating unjustly, i.e. someone who has a right not to be treated that way. Wrongdoing need not have a victim, but injustice must; the nearest in English to a rendering which used a similar word in both cases would be the contrast between 'wrongdoing' and 'wronging'. Socrates' whole line of argument for obligation to obey the law is going to be that the lawbreaker treats unjustly, or wrongs, the state or its laws, for which it is going to be no excuse that the state has, as he in fact insists that in his own case it has, first wronged him

(50c). Socrates' claim Οὐδαμῶς ἄρα δεῖ ἀδικεῖν (49b), if translated as 'In no circumstances then must one act unjustly',
together with his arguments that to break the law is (subject to
one qualification, to be brought in later) to act unjustly, gives
him his conclusion that one must not break the law. On the
other hand, the claim, if translated as 'In no circumstances then
must one do what is wrong' would not, together with the arguments, give the conclusion; for that the further proposition
would be needed that acting unjustly is always wrong. That is
to say, if Socrates were using as his starting-point a claim in
which ἀδικεῖν occurred in its general sense, it would in any case
require supplementation by a claim in which it occurred in its
specific sense, a supplementation which he does not in fact offer.
Furthermore, the text makes it reasonably clear that he is talking about, not wrongdoing in general, but wronging or treating
unjustly in particular. Two consecutive remarks by him in 49c
run:

(a) Τὸ γάρ που κακῶς ποιεῖν ἀνθρώπους τοῦ ἀδικεῖν οὐδὲν διαφέρει.

and (b) Οὔτε ἄρα ἀνταδικεῖν δεῖ οὔτε κακῶς ποιεῖν οὐδένα
ἀνθρώπων, οὐδ' ἂν ὁτιοῦν πάσχῃ ὑπ' αὐτῶν.

They translate as (a) 'For perhaps treating men badly does not
differ at all from treating them unjustly'

and (b) 'Then one must neither return unjust treatment to
any men nor treat them badly, no matter what treatment one
gets from them.'

In (a) κακῶς ποιεῖν should not, as in the translations it sometimes is, be rendered as 'injure', if that word is taken, as in the
absence of warning it will be, in its common, rather than its
technical, sense. In its common sense, if A by his conduct has
injured B, then B must by A's conduct have suffered some harm
or damage, for which for example he might in a civil suit seek
compensation. Contrapositively, if B has not suffered any harm
or damage, then A cannot have injured him. By contrast,
actual infliction of harm or damage (of whatever kind) is not
necessary to treating badly, nor to κακῶς ποιεῖν in Greek. If A
has made a promise to B, then by his mere failure to keep it he
has treated B badly, but he may not have done him any harm;
whether he has or not will depend on further contingent factors,

especially the extent to which B has relied on A's promise, and to which he will, for example, be out of pocket in consequence of his disappointed expectations of A's fulfilling his promise. By promising A *authorises* B to expect, and behaves badly towards him if he does not keep his word. The erroneous idea, to be found in legal and other textbooks, that by promising A *creates* an expectation in B stems from the failure to distinguish between authorising and creating an expectation, and encourages the confusion between treating a person badly and inflicting harm or damage on him. The present argument in the *Crito* is concerned with treating badly, not with inflicting harm or damage.

Taken in isolation, the remark in (a) that treating a man badly does not differ at all from treating him unjustly would naturally suggest that Socrates intends the two expressions as synonyms. But, when it is taken with (b), that suggestion falls. For, if the expressions were intended as synonymous, then the remark about *neither* treating a man unjustly (in retaliation for unjust treatment by him) *nor* treating him badly would be pointless; 'neither . . . nor . . .' would simply not be doing their work. (The same contrast is repeated with emphasis nine lines later.) So we have the puzzle how the two expressions should not be synonymous, while at the same time treating badly did not differ at all from treating unjustly. Socrates might mean that there was an equivalence between them, logical or material, or he might mean that treating badly could not be distinguished from treating unjustly, but without implying that treating unjustly could not be distinguished from treating badly. Any species-genus relationship will illustrate that; and it is caught in expressions of everyday English. A, hearing B boast of his success in taking money out of the church collection plate as it went round, might protest 'But, that's no different from stealing' or 'That's neither more nor less than theft', without implying that all there is to stealing, or that the only way there is of stealing, is taking money from a church collection plate.

Just what distinction Socrates had in mind we cannot tell for certain. But a possible conjecture would be that under the generic treating unjustly he is thinking of treating unjustly whether by treating badly or by damaging. Of the three arguments which he is going to use against disobedience to the law the first two are arguments from *treating badly*, the third an argument from *damaging*. Summarily, his case is going to be that *in* disobeying the laws a man treats them (or the state) badly, and (on one interpretation) that *by* disobeying the laws he damages them, i.e. that to disobey the laws both is to treat them badly and has as one of its consequences damage to the laws.

The principle that in no circumstances must one act unjustly is for Socrates absolute, and provides the foundation for his case on behalf of obedience to law. In persuading Crito to agree that they should concentrate solely on the issue whether they would be acting justly or unjustly in organizing and executing an escape for himself, and that they should disregard Crito's questions about cost, public opinion and the fate of Socrates' children, he maintains that, if it would be unjust, that would close the matter; they should not take into account that he must die if he stays. Nothing that he could suffer could count in comparison with what was unjust. This closely echoes (although, as will be shown, it does not *exactly* echo) his words in the *Apology* (28d), where he said that a man placed at his post by his commander should remain there and face the dangers, and that he should take into account neither death nor anything else in comparison with what is dishonourable. Where injustice is concerned, Socrates would not have approved of the way in which the U.S. Supreme Court has sometimes tried to come to terms with apparently absolute, and certainly awkward, clauses in the American constitution, viz. by considering balance of interests. For him it was not the case that in some circumstances one should act unjustly, but in others not; in no circumstances should a man act unjustly, if he could help it (49a). The prohibition was absolute and uncompromising: 'in no way must a man do what is unjust' (49b).

Incidentally, the claim here that a man should not act unjustly, if he can help it, might seem inconsistent with the more familiar Socratic paradox that nobody does what is unjust, if he can help it—on the ground that the former implies that it is possible to act unjustly, where one can help it, while the latter implies that it is not possible. But in fact there is no inconsistency, for the latter claim is a claim about knowledge, and

c

the lack of it: nobody can both know an act to be unjust and do it; for, if he knows it to be unjust, he must know what injustice is, and hence know that the act will be bad for himself, something which nobody could want; so, nobody could perform an act which he knew to be unjust. But he might perform one which he believed (even correctly) to be unjust; lacking the knowledge of justice he might not believe that performing the act would be bad for himself, and so he would lack the inhibiting belief (cf. *Meno* 77–8). So, a man *can* choose to act unjustly (i.e. to perform an act which he believes to be unjust); and consequently there is room for Socrates' prohibition here against so choosing.

Because the moral prohibition against injustice is absolute, it must be absolute too against repaying injustice with injustice; despite what most people think, to have been treated unjustly does not justify or excuse unjust action in return (49b); and similarly in the case of bad treatment (49c).

In 49e Socrates introduces a factor not previously mentioned. He poses it as a question asking for Crito's opinion, but that is clearly a device for expressing his own opinion; and it is one which is to play a major part throughout the remainder of the dialogue. It is that a man must do whatever he has agreed to do, provided that what he has agreed to do is right (or just) (49e). And what Socrates immediately suggests is that, if he leaves without first persuading the city to let him go, then

(1) he will be treating some people badly, those whom we should least treat like that,

(2) he will be failing to stand by an undertaking which he has given, where what he undertook to do was right (50a). And, he adds,

(3) he will be, for his part, destroying the laws and the whole city (50b).

Those are going to be his three reasons why a man must obey the law; they will be discussed below in each of Chapters Four to Six respectively. The elucidation of 'those whom we should least treat like that' in (1) is going to be that the laws stand to the subject in the relation of fathers to children, that fathers have rights in relation to their children which children do not have in relation to their fathers, and that his father's rights are the last ones a person should flout.

The argument under (2) is an anticipation of that later made familiar by the social contract theorists, that the obligation of obedience, in this case legal obedience, derives from an agreement having been given to obey. It should be noted that Socrates states the agreement principle, not in the bald form that a man is bound by his agreements, but in the form that he is bound by them provided that what he has agreed to do is right. Such a view is reflected in the modern legal principle that a contract is not legally binding if it has been made for an immoral or a criminal purpose, or if it is contrary to public policy. But, although Socrates deserves credit for avoiding the crude version of the agreement principle, he has thereby drastically weakened its force as an argument why a man must obey the law. That one should fulfil an agreement to obey the law, provided that what one has agreed to do is right, could at most provide a supplementary reason for the obligation to obey, it could not provide *the* or the *principal* reason. For one's obligation to fulfil the agreement to obey will depend on what one has agreed to do being right. But what one has agreed to do, according to the argument, is to obey the law. Therefore it must be independently established that it would be right to obey the law; *that* could not be established by appealing to the fact of the agreement and the claimed obligation to keep it. If that one has an obligation to keep the agreement which he has made to obey can be established only after it has been established that it is right to obey, then the agreement principle can be used only as reinforcement for the rightness principle; we need to know already that it would be right to obey. Socrates could have avoided the difficulty by making the obligation to keep the agreement to obey a defeasible obligation (as, in effect, it is in modern contract law): a man is bound by his agreements, *unless* what he has agreed to do is wrong. In fact, Plato avoids the difficulty by plunging back into the cruder, but more forceful, version of the agreement principle, that a man must do what he has agreed to do. The argument in 51d–53 depends on that, not on the qualified version of the formulation in 49e and 50a.

The objection to Socrates' use of the agreement principle developed in the preceding paragraph depends on understanding the principle in one of two jointly ambiguous ways in which it can be taken. It is the way which comes more naturally to mind, because it is the simpler, but we cannot be certain that it is the correct one, as we have no method of telling that Socrates (or Plato) was even aware of the ambiguity. The principle that a man should keep his agreements provided that what he has agreed to do is right can be taken in either of two ways:

(1) a man should keep his agreement to do x (where x is what he has agreed to do), provided that doing x is right.

(2) a man should keep his agreement to do x, provided that what he has agreed to do in agreeing to do x is right.

If we take the principle as in (1), and substitute 'to obey the law' for 'to do x' (and correspondingly for the other occurrences of x), we get the principle coming out as: a man should keep his agreement to obey the law, provided that obeying the law is right. The objection previously raised then holds: we would need to establish that it was right to obey the law, independently of having made any agreement to do so; the agreement principle, therefore, would be, at best, a reinforcing reason that we ought to obey the law.

On the other hand, if we take the principle as in (2), making corresponding substitutions, we get: a man should keep his agreement to obey the law if what he has agreed to do in agreeing to obey the law is right. What he has agreed to do in agreeing to obey the law is to conduct himself in specifiable situations in ways specified by those laws which apply to those situations. If obeying a particular law in a particular situation were (as it might be) wrong, then what he had agreed to do in agreeing to obey the law would in that situation be wrong, and he ought not to do it. He ought not in the situation to keep his agreement to obey the law, although (we may hope) in general he should, because in general what he has agreed to do in agreeing to obey the law is right.

The contrast between (1) and (2) can be brought out by assuming that doing x (here = obeying the law) *is* right. Then on (1) the man ought to do what he agreed to do, viz. obey the law, because the condition (both necessary and sufficient) of its being what he ought to do, namely that obedience to the law is right, is fulfilled. But on (2) what he has agreed to do in agreeing to obey the law *may* not be right, even though (as is being assumed) obedience to the law is right. In such a situation it will not be the case that he ought to do what he has agreed to do in agreeing to obey the law, even though he has agreed to obey the law, and though obedience to the law is right. In (1) he is incurring his duty of obedience to the law by a blank cheque, in (2) he is not.

Although we cannot be conclusively certain that the agreement principle appealed to in the *Crito* is (1) rather than (2), there is some reason to suppose that it is. In 50c the personified laws are represented as trying to convince Socrates that he should not allow his friends to engineer his escape from gaol, because (a) there was a particular law declaring that court verdicts were binding, and (b) Socrates had agreed to abide by court verdicts; he, therefore, ought to keep the agreement in his own case, even if the verdict had been unjust. The passage does accord with (1), if we substitute 'to abide by court verdicts' for 'to do *x*': Socrates should keep his agreement to abide by court verdicts, provided that abiding by court verdicts is right; and the laws have argued that it *is* right, because to do otherwise is to undermine law and state. It does not as readily accord with (2), which comes out as: a man should keep his agreement to abide by court verdicts, provided that what he has agreed to in agreeing to abide by court verdicts is right. What Socrates would have agreed to would have been to abide by the unjust verdict in his own case; and it is not clear that the provision that *that* be right had been met.

It might be argued that the qualification to the agreement, that it be just (or right), refers, not (as taken here) to whatever is agreed to, but to the nature of the agreement itself, that it must be justly made in circumstances which are just. The Greek in 49e–50a could stand that interpretation, which would give us an interesting forerunner of the Rawlsian justice as fairness. In 52e it is emphasised that the agreements between Socrates and Athens were not extracted from him by coercion, misrepresentation, or rushing him into a hasty decision; he had had seventy years in which it was possible for him to leave if the agreements did not seem to him to be just. That could be taken either way. It might mean: if the agreements did not seem to him to have been justly arrived at, because there had been some degree of coercion, or misrepresentation, etc. in arriving at them, although in fact there had not been. Or, it might mean: if the agreements did not seem to him to be just in their content, because there had been some degree of coercion, or misrepresentation, etc. in arriving at them, although in fact there had not been. There is no way of definitively settling the issue, but the interpretation adopted here is preferred, not merely because it seems the more natural way of taking 49–50, but also because it accords with Socrates' absolute principle that in no circumstances must one do what is unjust, whereas the alternative interpretation does not: a man might make a just agreement, i.e. one made in just circumstances (such as those specified in 52e), and one intended to produce a just outcome, but where it turns out that what he had agreed to was unjust.

In whichever version of the agreement principle, Socrates is advancing it, as he had his theses about injustice and about treating people badly, as an absolute, unexceptionable principle. Just as a man must in no circumstances do what is unjust, so he must do whatever he has agreed to do (at least, with the proviso that what he has agreed to do is right). So, if it can be shown that not to keep the law is unjust, or that one has agreed to keep it (and that what one has agreed is right), it follows, as he claims that it does, that he must obey the law. What Socrates never questioned was the alleged absoluteness of the obligation to refrain from acting unjustly, or of the obligation to fulfil one's legitimate agreements ('legitimate' is being used here to indicate the satisfaction of the provision that what one has agreed to do is right). Here many would want to disagree with him, for it does seem that no such obligation could be absolute or, without exception, morally binding. It is, unfortunately, true that human life is a messy business, with valid claims being sometimes in competition with one another, so that sometimes it is impossible to avoid doing injustice to somebody; or it may happen that the demands of social benefit may have to be preferred to those of justice. No doubt the reasons in favour of a course of action which involves treating some people unjustly have to be very strong before that course can be justified; and attempts to represent them as being very strong must be very carefully, even sceptically, scrutinised before they are to be accepted. But they can be strong enough for that; and, if they are, then what the agent is morally bound to perform is the action which involves some injustice, not the alternative action which avoids it. And similarly with legitimate agreements: we have a powerful obligation to keep them, but circumstances may unhappily arise in which the only right thing to do involves breaking a legitimate agreement. The issue is not as simple as Socrates makes it out to be. Even if it is true that we have agreed to obey the law, and even if it is thereby true that we have imposed on ourselves an obligation to obey it, it does not follow that the obligation is absolute and can admit of no exceptions. Although those in authority cannot be expected publicly to declare it, the civil disobedient who breaks a law out of the conviction that it is his duty to break that law is not necessarily being blind as to where his greatest obligations lie.

CHAPTER THREE

Duty to Avoid Injustice and Duty to Obey the Laws

Before moving on to consider Socrates' three kinds of reason why a man ought to obey the law, something should be said to avoid giving the impression that he was an uncompromising hardliner on the subject of legal obedience. First, we have to attend to a qualification which he several times stresses in the *Crito*. And, secondly, we have to compare what he says in that dialogue with the various things he had said in the *Apology*: there is at least a seeming discrepancy between his attitude in the one and his attitude in the other to the decision of a court of law; and in the speech for his defence in the *Apology* he both expresses some pride in his own defiance and maintains that there can be a higher call than the call of human law. Whether all of these elements can be worked into a single coherent account will have to be considered. At least it will emerge that, for all the moral emphasis which he places on fidelity to law, he has to allow that other things enter, or may enter, into the resolution of the question what a man ought to do, where there is no question what the law requires him to do.

The qualification in the *Crito* is stated, and then twice repeated, within the space of less than a page (51b–52a), so that it has to be taken as more than a passing remark. Socrates imagines the laws of Athens as personified, and as putting to him the case for obedience to them. Indeed, to say that he *imagines* them as personified is misleading, because at least the first two of the three arguments why he should not break the law depend upon the laws actually being in some sense persons. Precisely what is meant by 'the laws' (οἱ νόμοι) is not clear. Initially, he may be speaking as if there is some difference between the laws and the state; for he begins by saying 'Suppose the laws and [καί] the state were to come . . . and ask us' (50a). Or the καί might be explicative, rather than copulative, 'the laws, i.e. the state'. Later in their address the laws are represented as using 'the country', 'the city' and 'the laws' in ways which hardly seem interchangeable. For present purposes, how exactly he saw laws and state as related hardly matters; and it will not affect the argument if we regard them as identical. But his treating them as in some real sense, and not just fancifully, a person is important, and anticipates the view of the state as a person worked out in far more detail by Plato in the *Republic*.

As the arguments which the laws present for the obligation to obey are regarded by Socrates as overwhelming, we can refer to them as his arguments, even though he does not attribute them to himself. (A contrary view, that the arguments are not what Socrates himself accepts, but are what he believes a man of Crito's limited intellectual capacity will accept, should, despite its implausibility, be mentioned.)[1]

The qualification alluded to above is first stated in the following passage, and is here printed in italics: 'Or are you so wise that you have forgotten that your country is more to be honoured than your mother, your father, and all the rest of your forebears . . . and that you must respect and submit to . . . your country's severe treatment of you more than your father's severity, *and that you must either persuade it or do whatever it orders* . . .?' (51b)

Later in the same long sentence there occurs: '. . . but both in war and in the lawcourts and everywhere else you must do whatever your city and country orders, or you must persuade it in accordance with where justice really is' (51b–c).

Thirdly, at the beginning of the next page the laws represent themselves as moderate, 'proposing, and not harshly commanding a man to do whatever we order, but allowing him one or other of two choices, either to persuade us or to do as we say' (52a).

So, it is a part of being Athenian law to be reasonable, and to give the subject the option of persuading 'them' that what the law requires is wrong. That is nowhere further elaborated,

---

[1] Gary Young, 'Socrates and obedience', 19 *Phronesis* (1974), pp. 1–29.

and unelaborated it raises more questions than it answers. In its weakest form it would not be highly controversial, for it would be maintaining that in Athens people either must show what is wrong with a proposed law before it is enacted, or, if they are unable to convince the government or body proposing the legislation, then they must obey it after it is enacted. This sounds not unreasonable, provided that people do have a fair chance of influencing a bill before it becomes an act. But the principle would apply only in a democracy, and in a modern democracy only to an extremely limited extent. The people concerned will be, not all those to be affected by the law, not even the electorate, but just those members of the governed who are articulate enough to be able to make themselves heard and listened to by their legislative representatives. Persuading, as an alternative to obeying, will not be open to anybody not on the scene before the legislation. Those who arrive later, by birth or by immigration, will find themselves subject to laws the passage of which it was logically impossible for them to have prevented by persuasion; and that is true for most of us for most of the laws under which we live.

A stronger and more interesting form of the persuade-or-obey doctrine, which Socrates *might* have had in mind (and it would fit some of his attitude in the *Apology*), would be that which applied to existing law, not just to projected law; it would then include within its scope all those excluded by the weaker version. But—and this is the point of calling it the stronger form—it would permit some disobedience to law. For the doctrine says that a man is *either* to persuade *or* to obey, not that he must go on obeying until he can persuade the law that right is on his side. In effect, this form allows for the possible legitimacy of, at least, some civil disobedience, and it fits Socrates' polite but defiant challenge to the court in the *Apology*, 'I shall obey god rather than you' (29d). It is typical of civil disobedience that it attempts to change the mind of the government on the subject of a law or policy which by the civil disobedient's convictions is morally objectionable; and often it tries to change their mind by appealing over their authority to a public sense of justice or to a natural law violated by the offending law. Such a principled breaking of law is designed to persuade the people (if necessary) and certainly the government that a law or policy is wrong and needs changing. It was used by Gandhi against the British in India, and it was used by the civil rights movement during the 1960s against racial repression in the southern states of the U.S.A. Gestures such as blacks daring to sit at the front of the bus, or to drink from whites-only water-fountains, may have been less effective persuaders than their economic boycott of white-owned businesses, but they were carried out as part of a campaign of persuasion.

There is an objection to saying that the laws, in propounding the persuade-or-obey doctrine in that form would be allowing the possible legitimacy of civil disobedience, viz., that, if the laws of Athens provided for persuasion as an *alternative* to obedience in some circumstances, then persuasion in those circumstances would not *be* disobedience; it would be an exemption from a particular legal requirement provided by the law itself. However, it is the laws of Athens at the beginning of the fourth century B.C. that are being talked about, indeed it is they who, in the figure, are doing the talking; and we have no evidence at all that they did provide such exemptions, that obedience to law consisted in *either* persuading them (if a particular legal requirement was not right) *or* doing what the requirement demanded. If this stronger form of the persuade-or-obey doctrine were the one being propounded in this passage, it would be more plausible to understand the laws as declaring themselves ready to tolerate some disobedience in some circumstances, not always to take action against it. The possible legitimacy of civil disobedience would be preserved: it would be disobedience because not provided for by law, but obedience or penalty for disobedience might, as a matter of policy, not always be enforced by law.[1]

There is another aspect of persuasion which Socrates shows no sign of having thought of, but which anybody needs to think of if he is going to allow the legitimacy of persuasion as an alternative to obedience to an existing law. That is that 'persuade' (similarly Socrates' Greek word πείθειν) is, in Rylean terminology, a success word, and that, connected with that, the attempt to persuade, resulting in success or failure, takes time.

[1] Cf. Ronald Dworkin, 'On not prosecuting civil disobedience', *New York Review of Books*, vol. x, no. 11 (1968), pp. 14–21; reprinted in Ronald Dworkin, *Taking Rights Seriously* (London: Duckworth, 1977), pp. 206–22.

Parenthetically, some verbs, taken out of context, are ambiguous as between their success-use and their task-use. And Shakespeare knew how to exploit the ambiguity to make a joke:

Glendower: I can call spirits from the vasty deep.
Hotspur: Why, so can I, or so can any man;
  But will they come when you do call for them?

(I Henry IV iii. i. 53-5)

The persuade-or-obey doctrine, if taken literally, will be that it is all right to choose persuasion as the alternative to obeying the law, provided that you *do* persuade, that you win your case; but it is not all right if you do not. It is like telling a man that it is all right for him to take part in a race *only* if he wins it. Furthermore, while establishing that some requirement of law is wrong or unjust is not a contingent matter, persuading those whom you are trying to persuade that it is wrong or unjust is a contingent matter; and you may fail, not because what you say is false, nor because your argument is unsound, but because you are up against deaf ears, irrational or closed minds. It is not easy to accept the principle of the doctrine in this form, viz. that an act or program of principled disobedience is justified, if but only if it actually succeeds in changing the minds of those at whom it is aimed. At the time of action the agent may have no way of knowing whether it will succeed. He may, furthermore, have good reason to believe—and this is characteristic of most campaigns of civil disobedience—that success, if it comes at all, will be a long time coming.

Those difficulties could be avoided if instead of taking the persuade-or-obey doctrine literally, we were to interpret it as: *try* to persuade, or obey. The alternative to obedience is to undertake the task of trying to persuade the authorities that their law is bad or unjust; whether one succeeds in the attempt is another matter, and does not affect the justifiability of the attempt. But the trouble with that solution, which is most unlikely to have commended itself to Socrates, is that it is too easy, too permissive; it makes any disobedience at all to a law legitimate, only so long as it is a sincere and principled attempt to change the minds of those who have the authority to alter or repeal the law. A moral licence to break the law can hardly come at as low a price as that. But it is perhaps a moral licence of the right kind; only it should be made somewhat more difficult to get.

To elucidate this, let us turn to another aspect of the problem, indicated by an essential difference between morals and law, that there are no rules of morals (in spite of the way that many moral philosophers write), while there are rules of law, together with officials having the job of enforcing them, detecting breaches of them, and adjudicating alleged breaches of them. The problem of the legitimacy (under certain conditions) of disobedience to a law is understandably not the same to a subject and to an official of the system.

For the subject, if there seems to him to be a conflict between the moral claim of the situation in which he finds himself and the claim of the legal requirements, then he may have a problem, because, if he *feels* the claim of the legal requirements, as opposed to merely being aware that they are the legal requirements, then he feels that as itself a moral claim pulling against the other one. But, if the situation is such that it seems to him that it would be absolutely wrong to behave in the way required by law, e.g. because it is an unjustly discriminatory law, then he is not going to see himself as having a problem: the moral claim of the situation is a moral *demand*. That he sees things in that way leaves it, of course, still an undecided question whether he is correct in doing so, and whether he should be allowed or not to act according to his lights. But, unless the legal requirement must be always and absolutely binding, no matter what—and the claim that it must be is far too vulnerable to survive attack—then it must be possible for it to be true that the subject is correct. But, as living in society requires legal officials as the complement of those subject to law, we, even if not the subject, have to take the situation of the officials into account. Society depends on the system, and they have the function of making the system, or their own part of it, work. They will not be making it work if they license or tolerate absolutely any program of breaches of a law by subjects sincerely trying to persuade the authorities of the injustice of that law. Even if right and justice are on the side of the disobedient would-be persuaders, officials cannot be blamed for operating the rules of the legal system as they have undertaken and have been trained to do; they have a concern with the overall preservation of the system and its standards which the individual subject, caught up in his particular situation, does not have. And yet, while no society can survive systematic official tolerance of law-breaking persuaders, some index of the decency of a society is the extent to which it can and does tolerate them without endangering the system. For example, in many jurisdictions the rules of law are now being bent to accommodate euthanasia, and they will eventually be altered; and, on the other side of the ledger, often little good is done to the rule of law by mass arrests of demonstrators. That 12,000 such demonstrators were arrested in one city, Washington, D.C., on one day (May Day 1971) is something that many Americans with a respect for law would rather forget.

The suggestion that a decent society will be characterised by some degree of official tolerance of principled lawbreaking is more complex than has been indicated, because it is temptingly easy, but quite wrong, to think of civil disobedients as being always on the side of what oneself regards as that of sweetness and light. We have to make room among them for the convictions of those who see anti-discrimination laws as destructive of community, who want the restoration and extension of capital punishment, who want laws changed which, following U.N. resolutions, prohibit trade with white-ruled Rhodesia, etc.; we neither make room for them nor show why they should be excluded by calling their holders rednecks. If rednecks and bleeding hearts can be distinguished only by where their blood shows, we have no business trying to distinguish them. What are we to say about people who, holding views such as those instanced above, then engage in activities which are illegal under the laws to which they have principled objections? That is, what are we to say about how our officials should treat them by way of tolerating or not tolerating some principled lawbreaking? and about whether our officials are to be the judges of what tolerance is to be shown? The idea that a decent society will show some tolerance of lawbreaking by men convinced of the wrongness or injustice of the laws will not by itself discriminate between conscientious objectors trying to resist, protest or frustrate the operation of a draft law for providing wartime conscripts on the one hand and on the other hand businessmen opposed to economic sanctions against another country for its racial policies and attempting by every roundabout way that they can find to break the laws designed to enforce the sanctions, or policemen (or soldiers) who object to the protection given by law to a suspect brought in for interrogation, and who flout the law in every way that they can get away with. Either a decent society should as much tolerate lawbreaking by the one as by the other, or further relevant differences must be revealed. Somewhat analogously, American citizens who volunteered to fight in Angola or Rhodesia tended to be called mercenaries, Americans who flew for the Eagle Squadron in the R.A.F. in World War II were not; yet it is doubtful what constitutional difference there was between the one and the other.

First, we should have to distinguish between the pure and the impure lawbreakers. The pure are those who are convinced that it is right and their duty to break the law in question, not because, although in general a good law, it is in the present circumstances excusably or justifiably broken (e.g., breaking the speed limit to get an emergency patient to hospital), but because it is in its aim and usual operation and incidence a bad law (I omit the complication that the law to be broken may be, not the one which is objected to, but another, by the infraction of which the objected-to law is protested—e.g., breaking the law limiting the numbers allowed in a demonstration march, in order to protest the law being demonstrated against); who are motivated solely by their conviction that it is their duty to break the law; and who have nothing to gain themselves, in terms of profit or pleasure, by breaking it. The impure are those who fail to meet at least one of those conditions. If society is to tolerate some lawbreaking by them, it will be on grounds of convenience, rather than of decency. For there can be circumstances of convenience why some lawbreaking is better winked at than pursued: for example, if it is illegal for public employees to strike, but a very large number of them do, some political or economic solution may have to be found, with the illegality of the strike quietly forgotten, because the law's police and judicial machinery, by its design, is incapable of processing more than a few people at a time; and where the strike is solid enough, to pick out the, or some of the, strike leaders to be the few people will only make matters worse. Few student demon-

strators are pure disobedients; the pleasure of making themselves a nuisance to authority, say, by snarling up the traffic, or
of embarrassing authority by temporarily and defiantly
occupying authority's seat of power, is too great for that.
Businessmen can be sincere in condemning laws which prohibit
trade with Rhodesia, but few who get round the laws will be
uninspired by, or unrewarded by, the profits of trade. If there
is a reason for letting the impure disobedients go, it will be one
of convenience. But that still leaves the pure, the dedicated
freedom riders and the dedicated opponents of anti-discrimination laws who will do whatever they can to back their principles
by frustrating the laws. Is it a mark of a decent society that it
will show equal toleration of each? And should the decision
where principled lawbreaking is to be left alone, and how far,
be the decision of the system's own officials? The reply that a
decent society cannot be neutral, that it must, to some extent,
share the values of the lawbreakers whom it is judging, is a
partial, but not a complete, answer to the first question; there
is, unfortunately, little reason to doubt that the society of
Hitler's Germany shared to a considerable extent the values of
those who were persecuting Jews and other unwanted groups—
and would not have shared the values the less, had the persecution been illegal. The rest of the answer seems to be that we can
criticise a society for *what* it tolerates, not for its tolerating what
it does, for the values which it has, not for living by them. And
there cannot, in the abstract, be a satisfactorily complete
answer to the other question either: are the system's officials,
and if so which ones, to decide whether or not to prosecute?
The decision has to be a political, rather than a strictly legal,
decision, and whether it should be the law officers who decide
will depend on the nature of the system. One legal system will
itself be more political than another, e.g. the United States than
England, so that anticipated social benefits (minus costs) will
play more of a part in one than in the other. The widely held
theory that the role of the U.S. Supreme Court is to be in its
constitutional interpretation and rule-making responsive to the
expectations of the American people does make some kind of
sense in practice, although less than American piety claims for
it. It has more to do with reading and influencing trends than
it does with attending to public opinion polls. Similarly, when

in a decent society prosecuting authority suspects that the attitudes of the disobedients are not too far away from, and, in time at least, not too far ahead of its own, when it has some doubts, not about the law, but about the moral propriety of stigmatising them, it can afford to be generous. The risk that some disobedients' attitudes will be discordant with the decency of their society, but will not be perceived to be so by prosecuting authority, is one that simply will have to be taken.

The problem of principled disobedience, particularly of the kind raised by Socrates' persuade-or-obey doctrine, and exemplified by much civil disobedience, is much less the individual's problem ('What am I to do?') than it is the system's problem ('What are we to do about him?'). He may be right to go ahead and try to persuade by disobeying, but, even if he is right, that does not give him *a* right (even a moral right) to go ahead. For, for him to have that right the officials must have a correlative duty, viz. to let him go ahead and disobey the law; and that they have that duty is far from clear. In general, their duty is the opposite, to secure obedience, and convictions for disobedience; and that they do that already raises the price of a moral licence to pursue disobedience.

What this comes to is that a man may have been right in disobeying a law, while engaged in trying to persuade the authorities that the law should be changed; that his being right in that is not dependent on his being ultimately successful in persuading them; that his being right in engaging in such disobedience does not confer on him *a* right to engage in it, i.e. that the authorities do not have a duty to permit it; that, having the duty of maintaining the system, they have at least the *prima facie* duty of disallowing the disobedience to its current rules; but finally that there can be situations in which it is better that they allow some measure of such disobedience. Such situations are particularly those in which the current law, if rigorously imposed, treads on deep moral or religious convictions, whose holders' resistance evokes sympathy in the community.

We cannot extract all that from the bald persuade-or-obey assertions made to Socrates by the laws of Athens, and we cannot claim that that is what they or Plato meant. But it is an arguable position, which avoids both the severity of one extreme version of the doctrine (disobedience is permissible only

D

if you actually succeed in persuading), and the permissiveness of the other extreme (disobedience is permissible any time that you are trying to persuade). It allows that sometimes for the subject the duty to try to persuade by disobedience may be higher than the duty to obey, and that sometimes for the officials of the legal system it may be better not to pursue the disobedience. It would be obtuse to claim that the judgment when it is not to be pursued is easy to make; but only the hard-liner which Socrates shows himself not to have been would insist that it is never to be made.

The persuade-or-obey doctrine has so far been discussed as a doctrine about the duty of obedience to one's system's laws in general, for Socrates obedience to the laws of Athens. Another and perhaps more acceptable interpretation of the passage is that which makes it concern itself with the duty of obedience, not to the laws as such, but to specific orders made under law.[1] The difference would be instantiated in the contrast between the duty to drive one's car in accordance with current traffic law and the duty to halt it at a particular place and time as ordered by a particular policeman; if the rules of traffic law are orders at all (and arguably they are not), they are certainly of a very different kind from that policeman's order at that place and time. The alternatives presented by persuade-or-obey would be, then, not persuading policy makers or legislators not to enact a law, or to amend or repeal it, versus complying with the law, but persuading a legal officer, such as judge or policeman, who was making an order applying the law to a particular situation, not to apply it, versus obeying the order. This interpretation would fit well with 51, where the 'obey' option is twice specified as 'doing what your country orders', which includes quietly accepting whatever treatment it orders you to undergo, such as a beating or imprisonment, or being led out to war to face wounds or death. The one passage (52a) which cannot easily be read this way is that in which the laws remind Socrates that when they give orders they give them as proposals rather than as harsh commands. The trouble there is that what needs to be contrasted with a proposal is a command, not a *harsh* command. A command does not fail to be a command, if

---

[1] What follows is substantially owed to comments by Daniel Devereux.

it is given reasonably or humanely; it is still very different from a proposal. And we have no reason to believe that Athenian law permitted an appeal against every legal order before it had to be carried out. At the beginning of the *Laws* the Athenian stranger emphasises that, while the law gives an excellent lead to the citizen, it is also gentle (645a).

As there is a tendency among modern writers on civil disobedience to enrol Socrates among its pioneers, it should be pointed out that the question is too complex to be given a simple Yes or No answer. Socrates would not be on the side of modern civil disobedience, not because he was uncompromisingly on the side of obedience to law, but because there is not just one side of modern civil disobedience to be on or not on, but at least two sides; and Socrates, while he might have been on one of them, would certainly not have been on the other. (1) A man may feel the moral demand of a situation, where he finds the conduct which the law requires of him itself morally objectionable, i.e., it would be objectionable even in the absence of a law requiring it. The conduct required of him conflicts with obligations or principles which he has, and its claim cannot for him override theirs; that is the position, for example, of the conscientious objector who is not prepared to participate in war, or in *this* war, or in the taking of human life to promote policies or preserve liberties, however valuable they may be. His principles prohibit him from taking human life, and he therefore sees himself as having a principled duty to disobey a law which requires him to take it, or to assist others to take it. Americans who opposed their Vietnam war either on that principle or on other formally similar principles, with which the requirement that they, or other Americans, participate in the war conflicted, were, provided that in other ways they matched the description of a civil disobedient, civil disobedients of one kind. And they could legitimately claim to have Socrates as ancestor: not that he would agree that they had a duty to ignore or resist that particular requirement of law, that they answer their country's call to arms (he very likely would not agree), but he would seemingly agree that a man could have obligations which overrode the requirements of law. (2) On the other hand, a man might believe that he had a duty to disobey or to protest the law, not because what the

law required of him or others was objectionable, but because it
was objectionable that the law should require that—objectionable in a high degree, and in more than one possible way. Most,
if not all, of the civil disobedience of the civil rights campaign
in the U.S.A. during the 1960s was of this kind. Prohibitions
by state law from drinking at certain water fountains or sitting
in a certain section of the bus did not conflict with existing
obligations to drink from those fountains or to sit in that section
of the bus. They did not create situations of kind (1). What is
objectionable under heading (2) is either (a) that there should
be a legal requirement at all on such matters, or (b) what such
a requirement does to those who have to submit to it. Laws
curtailing artistic freedom or freedom of expression of ideas
would come under (a): they are objectionable because of the
value of what they frustrate. To the extent that it is possible at
all, civil disobedience by painters, writers and cultural dissi-
dents in general in the U.S.S.R. is of this kind; what they are
trying to protect is a valuable liberty, not a demanding obligation. Civil rights cases, on the other hand, belong overwhelmingly to (b). The duty of civil disobedience there was not to
submit to, or to save others from having to submit to, the
injustice of treatment under state law which insulted and de-
graded them as people. Nonconforming artists and intellectuals
in the U.S.S.R. have been victims, but not at all in the way that
those made the targets of racial discrimination have been. If
there is an obligation not to submit to being refused service at
a lunch counter because you are black, or to campaign against
such and other such treatment of blacks, it is not at all one
where the acts of obedience would themselves be wrong (there
is nothing wrong in not eating at such and such a diner or
drinking from such and such a fountain); it is the obligation
not to allow oneself or others to submit to being victims of a
certain sort. And to *that* kind of civil disobedience Socrates
would have given no support at all. The notion that one might
have a duty to disobey a law, in order to alter the injustice to
himself or to others, simply as human beings, of submitting to
it is a modern one. Socrates and Plato had some idea of self-
respect, but it was not the idea that gives a civil rights movement its hope.

Now let us turn to compare the *Crito* and the *Apology*, for there are apparent differences and discrepancies which have either to be explained or to be explained away. If, in each case, Plato is giving a substantially correct account of Socrates' views at the time, then more than minor discrepancies would be surprising, for biographically his trial and death, which the reported conversation of the *Crito* preceded by two days, were only a few weeks apart; and, although men do have death-bed changes of view, Socrates in the *Crito* emphatically denies that he has (46b). And yet, to give two examples, he does at least seem to be taking very different lines. First, in the *Crito* he says (or the laws of Athens say for him) that court decisions must be carried out, even if, as in his own case, both verdict and sentence were unjust (50b–c). On the other hand, in the *Apology* he had declared himself ready to ignore a certain decision if the court were to make it (29c–d). Secondly, in the *Crito*, as already discussed, the only situation in which he might be justified in disobeying the law was that in which he was engaged in trying to persuade the authorities that the law or the order under it was bad. In the *Apology* there is nothing about persuading; there is simply a higher call than the call to obey the law, namely the call to obey god and to avoid doing what is unjust (29–30). On that view a man must disobey the law when what it requires is unjust. The *Crito* view is that he *may* disobey, but not unless he is engaged in publicly protesting, or trying to persuade the authorities of, the injustice. Thoreau's refusal to pay his taxes might pass the *Apology* test, but would have to fail the *Crito's*— *if* they are as so far represented. A closer look at the relevant passages of each is needed.

Let us consider first the issue of compliance or non-compliance with a specific judgment of a court, which Socrates rightly recognises as being distinct from the issue of compliance or non-compliance with a law. A trial court, or court of first instance, in making an order is not making a law, it is (or should be) making an order under, or in application of, a law. The order is directed at the party (or parties) before the court, and at nobody else. If, for example, in granting a divorce a court gives custody of the children to the mother, then that is an order to just those persons concerned. A law, on the other hand, being general, applies to any members of the defining class: nobody may drive a car on the public highway except a

licensed driver; no will is valid unless its making conforms with
the requirements of the jurisdiction's testamentary law. The
distinction, which is that between *having the force of law* and
being law, tends to get blurred both by theories of law which
see all laws as commands and by theories (such as Kelsen's)
which use the same word 'norm' to refer both to a court ruling
and to the law under which it is made. A simple analogy in a
game is the distinction between a referee's decision on a particular incident (e.g. a free kick for off-side) and the rule which
he is there enforcing.

The argument in the *Crito* is that it would be wrong for
Socrates to escape from gaol, because that would be to nullify
the court's judgment, when it found him guilty and sentenced
him to death. Two different kinds of reason are given in support: (a) no state can survive in which court judgments have
no force but are cancelled out and destroyed by individuals
(50b); (b) there is a law of Athens declaring that all court
decisions are valid; and that is a law which Socrates has agreed
to abide by (50c). This is not yet the place to discuss the
strength of either of these two arguments, but it should be
pointed out that they are independent of each other (and consequently each will be discussed in separate chapters, Chapters
Six and Five respectively). Argument (a), that disregard of
judicial rulings is incompatible with a state's survival, does not
require as a precondition that people should have agreed to
obey the law. It is rather an argument of what might be called
the 'What would it be like if . . . ?' kind, and it can take either
an empirical form or an *a priori* Kantian form. The empirical
version would point out the consequences of people disregarding the verdicts, orders and other judgments of the courts
whenever they wanted to; it would result in the breakdown of
law and order and the collapse of the state. By analogy, think
what would become of a football game if everybody started
ignoring the referee. The Kant-type version would be an
argument, not from likely or certain consequences, but from
the conceptual impossibility of a legal system in which judicial
decisions had no efficacy. There could not *be* such a system, for
the idea of a legal system and the idea of judicial decisions being
inefficacious are mutually contradictory. By analogy, the arguments would be, not that a game of football in which the

referee's decisions were inefficacious would become a shambles (that was the argument in its empirical version), but that a 'game of football' in which the referee's decisions had no force just would not be a game of football. Whatever else the players were doing, they would not be playing football, for the notion of a game of football in which no attention is paid to the referee is inherently self-contradictory.

As mentioned above, this is not yet the time to assess the 'What would it be like if . . .?' doctrine, in whichever of its versions. But the games analogy suggests that it may not be totally invulnerable. It is not difficult to imagine how in some circumstances and given a certain kind of referee a particular match might actually be improved by ignoring him; the players might be more competent, or less corrupt, judges of their own conduct than he was. In some games, e.g. in golf as played by the top professionals, the standard of honesty in self-policing and self-judging is so high that the adjudicatory officials are almost dispensable.

Argument (b), on the other hand, does not depend either on the disastrous consequences of judicial decisions being ignored, or on the inherent contradiction of a legal system in which they were. Instead, it depends on the binding nature of agreement, if it is one entered into free from duress, fraud or the pressure of having to decide hastily (52e). The simplest case would be that in which two parties, being in dispute, agree on the choice of an arbitrator to give judgment between them, and agree in advance to accept his judgment, whatever it may be; each of them is morally bound by his agreement, even if the judgment, when given by the arbitrator, turns out to be unjust to him. Similarly, in the *Crito* the case is that Socrates is morally bound to accept the finding of the court, because he has agreed in advance to abide by the law which declares court decisions to be binding. If he is aggrieved by the personal injustice of the outcome, let him reflect that he has been wronged by men, not by the law (54b). If a man agrees to abide by a law declaring court decisions binding, then he does, and he must take the rough with the smooth. He cannot say afterwards, any more than in the example of arbitration, that the agreement holds only in those cases which work out for him, not for those which wrong him.

One could hardly get a more emphatic and unequivocal statement of the citizen's obligation to abide by a court finding than that made in the *Crito*. What of the *Apology*? In the crucial passage there (29c–d) Socrates might seem to be doing the exact opposite, and to be defying the court. He imagines them telling him that they are not going to listen to the prosecutor and that they are discharging Socrates, but with the provision that he no longer spend his time in his previous pursuits and in philosophising; if they catch him at it again, he will die. And to that he says that he would reply: 'I shall obey god rather than you, and so long as I draw breath and retain the capacity I shall never desist from doing philosophy, nor from both exhorting you and demonstrating to whomever of you I run into from time to time . . .' It is easy to read the passage thus, as, on the one hand, the court making an order (Socrates is to abide by certain terms of his release—he is not to continue philosophising), and, on the other hand, Socrates declaring that he would not obey such an order (he would continue philosophising just as he had before the trial); and, if that is the correct reading, then there is a remarkable conflict between Socrates' attitude at the trial and his attitude four weeks or so later. But, in fact, we do not have to read the text that way. First, although the story is one about a court *decision* (to release Socrates), it is far less clearly one about a court *order* (Socrates is not to continue philosophising). What the court actually says is that they are releasing Socrates, provided that . . . The condition which the court imposes is not a condition for freeing him, but a condition for leaving him free afterwards. It cannot be a condition of freeing a man that he conduct himself in a certain way *after* he has been freed, but that can be a condition of his continuing to be free. It might have been made a condition of releasing Socrates that he undertook (before release) that he would refrain from his old activities; but there is absolutely nothing in the text about that. In effect, what the court would be doing, on this reading, is releasing Socrates, but warning him that, if he is caught at his old activities again, he would be rearrested and eventually put to death; and Socrates would be replying that he would ignore the warning. Ignoring a warning, or announcing one's intention not to fulfil a condition of being left at liberty are not the same thing as disregarding an order; and there would thus be no inconsistency with the line taken in the *Crito*.

In Greek, as in English, the idiomatic use of grammatically conditional terms, although untroublesome to those familiar with the idiom, could be bewildering to the excessively literal-minded. 'We release you, on condition that you behave yourself afterwards', unless one tries to insist that it says something which is logically impossible (i.e., 'If, after we have released you, you behave yourself, then we release you') is no odder than other, variously different, idiomatic uses of 'if': e.g., 'There is milk in the refrigerator, if you want it', 'If I remember right, he was wearing a blue tie with red stripes', and the philosopher's friend 'I can, if I choose'.

What gives some credibility to the interpretation according to which the court would be making an order, with which Socrates would be declaring that he did not intend to comply, is that Socrates begins his reply by saying that, while he has a high regard for the court, yet πείσομαι μᾶλλον τῷ θεῷ ἢ ὑμῖν, which is often translated as I translated it above, viz. 'I shall obey god rather than you'; and 'obey' naturally suggests that it is an order that is being responded to. Now, the Greek verb πείθεσθαι (which is the middle or the passive voice of πείθειν, discussed earlier in this chapter), although it often does mean 'obey', does not always; it ranges over a wide field of related senses. Only five lines earlier than the present occurrence it had been used (negatively) to mean that the court would not follow the prosecutor's recommendation that they return a verdict of guilty; it would be absurd to talk of a court *obeying* a prosecutor (or a defendant). And four pages earlier it occurs in a passage where it has to mean 'believe' or something close to it ('I do not believe you on this, Meletus . . .' or 'I do not take your word for this, Meletus . . .'—25e). In fact it can mean anything that corresponds in the passive to the active 'persuade': 'be persuaded', 'be guided by', 'believe', 'believe in', 'trust', 'obey', etc. We are not compelled to read Socrates as here refusing to obey a court order, he could as well be declaring that he would not be persuaded by them, that he would disregard their condition for leaving him at liberty. And, as the latter interpretation, while doing no violence to the text, also avoids inconsistency with the *Crito*, it has much to recommend it. This solution to the apparent discrepancy between the passages in the *Apology* and in the *Crito*, although somewhat similar to one I proposed some years ago,[1] is not identical with it; it is simpler and, I now think, preferable.

It is true that Socrates does think of himself as being subject to the orders of god, but we cannot infer from that that he was unable to distinguish between a court of law ordering him not to behave in a certain way and the court informing him, by way of warning, what would happen to him if he did. There is indeed a theory of law, sometimes known as American Realism, and now happily discredited at least outside American law schools, according to which statements of law are hypothetical statements informing a man what the courts will, or probably will, do to him if he is caught behaving in a certain way. On this view, what may look like orders or prohibitions are really conditional predictions. But we have no reason to suppose that Socrates was similarly unable to discriminate between an order and a conditional prediction. We therefore have to choose between interpreting the court as ordering him to refrain from his philosophical activities, and interpreting it as telling him what would happen to him if he were caught still at them; and the latter interpretation has been recommended. His situation would not be formally similar to that of Antigone who knowingly disobeyed Creon's edict forbidding the performance of burial rites for her dead brother Polyneices, and who answered Creon's accusation with the reply that the laws of man cannot override the laws of the gods (Soph. *Antig.* 449–55).

We must now turn to the wider question of obedience to law in general, as treated in the *Apology* and in the *Crito* respectively. Certainly there is some difference in emphasis between the two, but is there more than that? As we have seen, in the *Crito* the only permitted alternative to obedience is persuading, or trying to persuade, the authorities that the law in question is in some respect bad. Socrates nowhere claims that persuading somebody that something is the case entails that it *is* the case—and indeed it does not entail it. But it fits his general line of argument to suppose that he was thinking only of that persuasion

[1] A. D. Woozley, 'Socrates on disobeying the law', in Gregory Vlastos (ed.), *The Philosophy of Socrates* (Garden City, N.Y.: Doubleday-Anchor Books, 1971), pp. 299–318.

where what the other party is being persuaded to believe (if the attempt is successful) is in fact correct. For instance, it accords with his view that we must keep our agreements, provided that what we have agreed to *is* right or just; and, closer to the present topic, he represents the laws as criticising the man who, having promised to obey them, does not, in the words 'he neither obeys us nor persuades us, *if there is something we are not doing* well' (51e, my italics; cf. 51c). In the *Apology*, on the other hand, the emphasis is on refraining from doing what is wrong or unjust, even though that involves disobedience; nothing is said about the disobedience being designed to persuade the authorities that what is required by obedience is unjust.

These are Socrates' words in the *Apology*:

(a) 'Wherever a man posts himself, thinking it is the best place for him to be, or wherever he is posted by a commander, there he must, as it seems to me, stay and face the risks, taking no account either of death or of anything else as against what is disgraceful' (28d).

(b) 'I then would have done a terrible thing if where my commanders had stationed me . . . I remained at my post and risked death, but when god appointed me, as I believed and supposed, to the task of a life of doing philosophy and examining myself and others, then I were through fear of death or anything else to desert my post' (28e).

(c) 'But to do what is unjust and to disobey one who is better than myself, whether he is god or man, that I know to be bad and disgraceful' (29b).

The military figure in (a) and (b) recurs in the *Crito*, and is not in the first instance, either there or in the *Apology*, metaphorical. Socrates is talking literally of the soldier in battle, and incidentally in the *Apology* is reminding the court, by way of counteracting the smear of his disloyalty to Athens, that he had won a reputation for his personal courage as a soldier in defence of Athens on several occasions during the Peloponnesian War. It becomes a metaphor when he transfers it to god and to the law.

Nowhere in (a) or (b) does he say that one should *never* disobey orders; what he says is that one should never disobey through personal fear. That obedience brings with it the risk, or even, as in Socrates' actual case in the *Crito*, the certainty, of death is never a good enough reason for disobedience. On the other hand, if disobedience involves doing what is disgraceful (as it is, for example, if the commander is better than the commanded), then that is always a good enough reason for *not* disobeying; against what would be base or dishonourable nothing else is to count. This too is repeated in the *Crito*, where he insists that a man should let anything happen to him rather than do what is unjust (48d).

Socrates' language indicates that disobedience might involve doing what is disgraceful in either of two ways: a man might do what is disgraceful *by* disobeying, or he might do it *in* disobeying. He would do the first if the act which he performed, disobeying orders in doing it, were itself disgraceful, e.g. running away from danger in battle (*Apol.* 28d). Whatever is to be said about running away in respect of its being in disobedience to orders, it is disgraceful as an act of cowardice. The man would do the second if the act were one of disobedience of a kind which is itself disgraceful, e.g. disobeying the orders of someone better than himself (*Apol.* 29b). Whatever is to be said about the act, say, as act of running away from danger, it is disgraceful as an act of disobedience to a being (whether man or god) better than himself. Also in the second category would fall the disgrace of disobedience, where it was disobedience through fear (*Apol.* 28e). So, cowardice is disgraceful, cowardice in disobedience to orders is doubly disgraceful, cowardice in disobedience to orders by one better than himself is triply disgraceful. Prudent and rational retreat from danger would not be disgraceful, in disobedience to orders it might not be, in disobedience to orders of one better than himself it would be.

It is to be noted that in both (a) and (b) above Socrates explicitly introduces an element of subjectivity into the basis of moral judgment: what a man ought to do or refrain from doing, depends on what he himself believes about the situation. In (a), if he believes that it is best that he should take up the position that he has, then he must stay there at all costs. In (b), if he believes that god has appointed him to a certain task, then he must stay with it at all costs. Although the phrase in (a) about a man being assigned to his post by somebody under

whose command he is (ἢ ὑπ' ἄρχοντος ταχθῇ), *might* be unquali-
fied by the phrase about belief (ἡγησάμενος βέλτιστον εἶναι), it
is better to read it as so qualified. Otherwise, Socrates would be
committing himself to the view that a man should do whatever
a higher officer orders him to do, that it is always an adequate
defence to a charge of having done what was wrong that one
was carrying out orders. And *that* is a view which he certainly
rejected; four pages later he refers to an episode in his own
career when he deliberately disobeyed a government order,
and precisely on the ground that what he had been ordered to
do was immoral. And there again he uses the same contrast as
in (a) and (b): '. . . I showed . . . that about death . . . I did
not care at all, but that doing nothing either unjust or wicked
counted for everything' (32d). It is not disobedience to orders
as such that is absolutely unacceptable, but disobedience where
it involves what is base, unjust or wicked.

For that reason, to translate in (c) the words τῷ βελτίονι as
'my superior' (as does Hugh Tredennick in his Penguin version) is unfortunately misleading, because it gives the impression that Socrates there *is* saying that it is bad to disobey one's
superior officer. What he is condemning is, not disobedience to
one who outranks him, but disobedience to one who is better
than he is. Being better than is a proper meaning of 'superior',
but not in the context of obedience or disobedience to orders.

That a man should never do what is unjust, no matter what
the refusal costs him personally, even the loss of his life, is one
of the main themes of Socrates' defence in the *Apology*. And by
an ironic, but not inconsistent, twist to the argument he cited
that as the reason which made him stay out of political life in
Athens: if he had entered, his principle would have required
him to do everything he could to oppose and prevent the many
injustices and illegalities perpetrated in any democracy; and
he would have been done away with long before he could have
achieved any good either for the city or for himself. The only
way for a man who really wants to fight for justice, if he proposes to survive even for a short time while doing it, is to lead a
private life and keep out of public affairs (31–2).

In fact, Socrates had played a brief and limited part in
public life, and he cited two incidents from it, to show that he
had in practice lived up to his principle that, when faced with

the choice between doing and refraining from doing what is unjust, one must always refrain. In the first incident he had been the only member of the then executive or presiding committee (consisting of fifty members) of the council of Athens to oppose, and to vote against, holding a collective trial of ten naval commanders accused of neither recovering from the sea the bodies of the dead nor rescuing the survivors from the vessels sunk in the victorious battle of Arginusae in 406 B.C. (Strictly, Socrates was not the only opponent of the collective trial. Other members of the committee opposed it too on the ground that it was, by Attic law, unconstitutional. But feeling in Athens against the commanders ran so high, and pressure on the committee became so great, that the other members dropped their opposition. Socrates was the only hold-out, the only one who refused to compromise principles under pressure. The full description in Xenophon *Hellenica* i. 7 brings out the strength of Socrates' conviction and character even more clearly than does Socrates' own brief account in the *Apology*.)

Socrates' opposition had nothing to do with the question of the commanders' guilt or innocence (and the facts in the case were seriously in dispute), but wholly with the injustice of depriving each of them of his constitutional right to an individual trial; and he emphasised that, even though the speakers in the assembly were ready to indict him and bring him to trial, and the assembly were shouting and egging them on, yet he thought that he must, whatever the risk, stay with the law and with justice (32b–c).

Presumably his view was, not that abstract justice demanded that the commanders should be given individual trials, but that, because constitutional law required that they should, justice demanded that that law be adhered to. Is Socrates, then, implying here that *any* violation of the law is unjust, and must therefore be refrained from? Is he committing himself to the view that the law must always be obeyed? The answer is No; and, to explain the answer, some distinctions have to be drawn.

It is the repeatedly emphasised view of the *Apology*, as of the *Crito* too, that one must never do what is unjust. But he does not clearly commit himself in the *Apology* (as arguably he does in the *Crito*) to the view that all illegal acts are unjust. Certainly, in fact, they are not. For it is possible for a law itself to be unjust, and in quite a variety of ways. For example, a law can make unjust discriminations, and conduct which fails to observe those discriminations will accordingly be illegal; but it might be just. If a law required a woman's rates of pay to be lower than a man's, where their work, skill and output were the same, an employer might see that the claims of justice conflicted with the claims of law. The Socrates of the *Crito* might argue that the employer was unjust to the law in breaking it, but he could hardly argue that all the injustice was on one side.

There are two peculiarities of the Arginusae case, each of which makes unsound a generalisation from Socrates' stand on it to the view that it is always unjust or, more widely, wrong for the subject to disobey the law. First, the law in question was not substantive law, but procedural law, and law for a special procedure at that, viz. the procedure for the conduct of a criminal trial with a capital sentence. No doubt, the presumption of innocent until proved guilty sits more happily today than it did then, the more so when a public trial was held, not before a small and carefully screened jury, but in a full assembly of volatile Athenians. But Socrates would acknowledge that, when a man is to be brought to trial on a criminal charge, and a capital charge at that, justice demands that the constitutional rules of trial procedure, designed to secure a fair trial, should be scrupulously adhered to. Justice demands that every man equally be given a fair opportunity of defending himself, and that, where the law provides that opportunity, that law should be observed. It is more important that the laws of adjudication be not broken than that the laws being adjudicated be not broken; and one cannot extrapolate from the proposition that trial law should not be disobeyed the conclusion that no law should ever be disobeyed. Secondly, the choice for Socrates over the Arginusae trial was not whether or not he as a subject would adhere to the law, but whether or not he as a legal official would adhere to the law. As one of the presidents of the court it was his job to see that the legal requirements of trial procedure were adhered to. From its being wrong, and unjust to a defendant, that a court official should not uphold trial law one cannot extrapolate the conclusion that it is wrong for anybody ever to disobey any law. It may be wrong, but one cannot argue from the standard to be expected of an official whose duty it is to uphold the law that the same standard is to be expected of the subject; their responsibilities in relation to the law are not the same.

The interest of the second incident which Socrates relates, in which he disobeyed a government order to go with four others and bring in a man for execution, is that he nowhere describes the order as being *illegal*. Xenophon (if we are to take the passage as authentic) says that the order was illegal (*Mem.* IV. 4. 3). Socrates' account of the episode is in marked contrast with the immediately preceding account of the Arginusae case. There he had stressed three times in six lines the illegality of the court procedure, and he recalled the subsequent decree of the assembly declaring that the trial had been illegal (by that time the six commanders who had stood trial had been executed). But in the story of the arrest of Leon of Salamis the word νόμος (law) is not used once. All the emphasis is on the wickedness of the government of the Thirty, on their attempts to implicate as many as possible besides themselves in their evil conduct, and on Socrates' resolution not to be overwhelmed by them, powerful as they were, into doing anything that was ἄδικον or ἀνόσιον, i.e. either unjust to men or sinful against god (32c–d). As there is no doubt at all that he believed that he was justified in ignoring the government's order, it is tempting to suppose that he is claiming that a conscientious refusal to obey the law *can* be right, viz. where what is required by the law is unjust action. Where there is a conflict between the claims of justice and legal fidelity justice must prevail. And the coupling of justice with right conduct in relation to god must not be ignored, for it was one of the main themes of Socrates' defence at his trial that he had been led by the voice of god, and that obedience to god must have priority over all else. Furthermore, the claim that a man must never do what is unjust provides the basis in the *Crito* of the arguments for his obligation to obey the law; the obligation never to do what is unjust is there uncompromisingly absolute (49a–b). What then, if a law requires one to do what is unjust? The only answer Socrates could consistently give would be: disobey—thereby opening a defence for civil disobedience.

But it is not entirely clear that he actually does give that answer. And, if he does, a question arises about consistency between the *Apology* and the *Crito*, which appears also as a question about internal consistency within the *Crito* itself. Each of these points must be examined.

First, while for us the contrast between the requirements of law and those of morals is reasonably clear cut, it may have been less so for an Athenian of the fifth or fourth centuries B.C. Overwhelmed as we are today by the growth of legislation and adjudication we tend to think of law in terms of positive law, whereas the Greek word νόμος was considerably wider in its scope. It is true that νόμος was sometimes, especially when contrasted with φύσις, thought of, and indeed somewhat disparagingly thought of, as a matter of human convention as opposed to what was so independently or by the nature of things.[1] Thus, Aristotle reports some people as believing that beauty and justice exist νόμῳ only, not φύσει (*NE* 1094b16); and in the *Protagoras* Plato has one of his characters refer to νόμος as 'mankind's tyrant, which does much violence against φύσις' (337d). But this was a deviation from the general trend, to be found running through the poets, tragedians and prose writers alike, which was to use the word νόμος much closer to the later notion of natural law, comprehending the usages and institutions of fundamental, sometimes unwritten, law (the later Plato had some reservations about admitting unwritten law to be law at all, cf. *Laws* VII. 793); and in Athens the νόμοι were in general contrasted with ψηφίσματα, which were the enacted laws, so that Demosthenes could write of 'the νόμοι in accordance with which the ψηφίσματα must be drawn' (485.3). Sophocles uses the word νόμος to mean a principle or rule of conduct (*Antig.* 191). In the *Hippias Major* Socrates asserts that when those who try to make law fail to achieve the good, they fail to make law (284d). This distinction, between law as it really is and law as enacted, is not to be confused with another distinction which Plato quite properly recognised, viz. that between law and statute, e.g. that between marriage law and the statutes embodying it (*Laws* IV. 721). 'What is the present law of divorce in Britain?' is not the same question as 'What are the current statutes on divorce in Britain?'

[1] Cf. J. Walter Jones, *The Law and Legal Theory of the Greeks* (Oxford: Clarendon Press, 1956), pp. 34–6; Trevor J. Saunders, 'Antiphon the Sophist on Natural Laws (B44DK)', *Proceedings of the Aristotelian Society*, 1977–8.

E

John Burnet has suggested in his *Early Greek Philosophy* (Introd. vi) that the use by early cosmologists like Anaximander of moral and legal terms in explaining the changes of seasons of the year was natural enough at a time when the comparative orderliness and lawfulness of human social life were more easily apprehended than the uniformity of nature. The doctrine of natural law had been given clear expression by Heracleitus in one of the surviving fragments: 'All human νόμοι are nurtured by the one divine νόμος' (DK 22B 114). This was thought to account for the similarity of unwritten law from one place to another, where absence of a common language would have prevented the same laws being established everywhere by human convention (Xenophon *Mem.* IV. 4. 19).

Consequently, while Socrates should have had no difficulty in allowing either that a ψήφισμα or an executive order might require a man to do what was unjust, it is perhaps less certain that he would have said the same thing of a νόμος; and νόμος is the word used uniformly throughout both the *Apology* and the *Crito*—ψήφισμα (which Plato does sometimes use in contrast to νόμος; cf. *Theaet.* 173d, *Laws* 920d) does not occur in either work. His outright disobedience to the order of the Thirty he probably would not have seen as disobedience to law. While the initial appointment of the Thirty to be the government of Athens following final defeat in the war had been legal enough, their administration became more and more arbitrary and tyrannical, any pretence of justice in the conduct of trials for crimes against the state was abandoned, and more and more citizens who were, or might be, in opposition to their wickedness were put to death. In the eight months that their rule lasted before they were themselves deposed they showed that there was little that they could have been taught in the way of repression by their twentieth-century descendants, the government of Greek colonels. It would have been impossible for Socrates to believe that in disobeying their order to bring in a man for summary execution he was disobeying the law. So, the episode did not represent for Socrates a conflict between fidelity to justice and fidelity to law. The Thirty were the lawfully appointed government, but their conduct and orders were not lawful. He did not *say* at his trial that their order to him was contrary to νόμος, because he did not need to; their brief but

bloody reign of terror had been so universally condemned that
there was no point in his claiming that what they had ordered
him to do was contrary to law; nothing was to be gained by
reminding the court of that.

When a modern writer proposes to deny the identity for
Socrates of what is just and what is law, he should remember
that he is writing in modern terminology, not in Socratic nor
Attic terminology.[1] He needs to bear in mind the distinction
between what might be called real laws and actual laws respectively, a distinction to which Socrates' views committed him,
even if he did not always and clearly observe it. If the recollec-
tions recorded by Xenophon are to be depended on, there is a
useful statement of Socrates' identification of the just with the
lawful in *Mem.* IV. 4. Of course, actual laws can be unjust, and
the problem of obedience to them remains. In what follows,
'the law', 'laws', etc. should be understood as meaning the
actual law, laws, etc. But it has to be admitted that, while this
makes philosophical discussion of the *Crito* tidier, it may give a
not entirely accurate, because overprecise, reading of Socrates'
arguments.

On the evidence of the *Apology* alone the case for maintaining
that Socrates anywhere in it argues that disobedience to the
law can be justifiable is weak. And yet perhaps the consistency
between it and the *Crito* is achieved only by a technical point.
In the case of the imagined release of himself from the charge
brought against him by Anytus (29c–d) he does not declare
that he would disobey the court, because he does not represent
the court as giving him an order. But it is impossible to believe
that, if the court had actually ordered him to discontinue his
previous philosophical activities (as opposed to warning him
what would happen if he did not), he would not have declared
his intention of disobeying them. His reason for disregarding
the warning would have been strong enough for disobeying a
court order—unless, as in the *Crito*, the fact that it was a court
order, and as such had the backing of a νόμος, would have made
the difference. We cannot tell. If we did not have the *Crito*, we
would have no reason at all for doubting that Socrates would

---

[1] Rex Martin, 'Socrates on disobedience to law', 24 *Review of Metaphysics*
(1970), pp. 23–4.

have been prepared to disobey a court order to discontinue doing philosophy. But we do have the *Crito*, and we have to choose between bringing it in in aid and admitting a discrepancy in attitude between the two works towards at least one kind of disobedience. The notion that the Socrates of the *Apology* would have said to the court that, if they were giving him an *order* to stop philosophising, that made all the difference, does take some swallowing; so, on the other hand, does the notion that there would have been such a discrepancy between his attitude at the trial and his attitude in the death cell a few weeks later, and yet that he neither noticed it nor pointed it out himself.

There are those who argue that even in the *Crito* Socrates does not mention that a man should always obey the law (subject to the admitted qualification of persuasion). Francis Wade contends that the principle of no disobedience is modified by two other principles enunciated by Socrates:[1] (a) in no circumstances should one wrong or harm anoteer; and (b) one's obligation to keep agreements is subject to the provision that they are just. For Socrates to obey the court in the *Apology* (Wade takes it to *be* an order) would be for him to harm the god; therefore he should not obey. And that conclusion is unaffected by bringing in from the *Crito* the court order *there* on the ground that it falls under the law validating all court orders, that being a law which Socrates has agreed to obey. The conclusion is unaffected, because agreement to obey a law is binding only where what is agreed to is just; what Socrates would be doing in obeying the court order in the *Apology*, viz. disobeying the god, would be unjust; therefore the agreement to obey the law validating court orders would not be binding in the case of the *Apology* order. On the other hand, it is binding in the case of the *Crito* order (that he carry out the death sentence on himself), because there the law is requiring him, not to perform injustice, but to suffer it himself; and if he does not obey he will be treating the laws unjustly.

Such an interpretation is ingenious, and no doubt catches much of the spirit of Socrates. But, as we are wholly dependent

[1] Francis C. Wade, S.J., 'In defense of Socrates', 25 *Review of Metaphysics* (1971), pp. 311–25.

on a text, we had better pay more careful attention to the letter. (In what follows, where Wade uses 'harm' I prefer, for the reason given in Chapter Two, pp. 19–20 above, an expression like 'treat badly'. The idea of a man treating his god badly, behaving badly towards him, is compatible with a man being unable to harm gods, which as Gene James has rightly pointed out, Socrates at *Euthyph.* 13c fairly clearly implies to be the case.)[1] The principle that a man should do whatever he has agreed to do, provided that it is just, which Socrates enunciates twice (49e–50a), has to be understood as supplying a condition which is both necessary and jointly with other conditions mentioned sufficient for the obligation to stand by an agreement; if it only completed a sufficient condition, the question what a man's obligation would be if what he had agreed to were not just would be left open. But nobody reading the text can plausibly suppose that Socrates was leaving it open, so we can agree with Wade in taking Socrates to be denying that a man has an obligation to keep an agreement if it is unjust.

But the referent of the 'it' is important. A man must do what he has agreed to do, provided that *what he has agreed to do is just*. What Socrates has agreed to do is to obey the laws, and in the particular case the law declaring the validity of court decisions; and it might be that obedience to the law was just (to the laws) at the same time that obedience to a court decision under the law was unjust (to the party involved in the case). It may well be that Socrates would have accepted Wade's reconciliation between the *Crito* court decision and that in the *Apology* (if it had been one), but only by his failing with Wade to attend to the difference of level between laws and decisions analogous to that between rules and acts familiar to students of utilitarianism. Wade throughout presents Socrates as concerned with the question whether in implementing the court decision he will be acting justly or not. What the principle of agreement to obey the law, if what one has agreed to do is just, requires is that Socrates be concerned whether he will be acting justly in obeying the law declaring the validity of court decisions.

The further argument that there is no inconsistency between

[1] Gene G. James, 'Socrates on civil disobedience and rebellion', 11 *Southern Journal of Philosophy* (1973), p. 123.

disobedience to the court in the *Apology* and obedience to the court in the *Crito*, because in the first Socrates is being told to *act* unjustly, but in the second to *suffer* injustice himself, is hardly convincing. First, Socrates nowhere says anything about *others*, i.e. acting unjustly to *others* and treating *others* unjustly. What he does say is that one must in no circumstances act unjustly, do what is bad, treat people (ἀνθρώπους) badly (49b–c)—not even in retaliation for unjust or bad treatment received. In the case of retaliation, clearly, another is involved; and, in general, when a man wrongs somebody or treats him badly, the somebody is somebody else. But he does not *have* to be. General moral judgments are person-neutral, and a man *can* treat himself badly. If the death sentence on Socrates was unjust, and as the method of execution was by self-administration, it is not far-fetched to say that he would be acting unjustly to himself in carrying it out. Furthermore, as argued in the *Phaedo* (62c), for Socrates to take his own life would be to treat the gods badly, because it is not for us, being the possessions of the gods, to decide what is to become of us. What will save his death by self-administered poison from being impious (impiety being that which in relation to the gods corresponds to injustice in relation to men) is that it is a necessity imposed on him by divine decision itself. There is no mention in the *Crito* of the gods deciding that Socrates should die; but, if we are allowed to bring in the *Phaedo* passage in aid, then the contrast between defiance of the court in the *Apology* and submission to it in the *Crito* rests, not so much on the distinction between doing injustice and suffering it, as on the proposition that to do otherwise in either case would be to disobey god.

It is worth noting that Plato's final view on suicide is much more humane than the view given in the *Phaedo*. In *Laws* 873c–d suicide is still to be regarded as a shameful act, but exceptions are allowed, in addition to the earlier one of being in obedience to a legal order of the state: it is to be excused if it is the response to an agonising and unavoidable blow of fortune, or if the person has shared in a disgrace from which there is no way out and which cannot be lived with.

Furthermore, it should be remembered that the argument for obligation to obedience based on agreement to obey is only one of three arguments which Socrates advances against disobedience, and that the limiting condition, viz. that what one has agreed to be just, is not mentioned in either of the other two arguments. In the case of the argument from the laws as parents Socrates may have thought that he was bringing it in when he allowed as an alternative to obedience persuading the laws in accordance with where justice lies (51c). But, at most, that is to permit disobedience to injustice, not to require it; and, as pointed out earlier, the alternative there to obedience is not disobedience simpliciter, but persuasion or attempt to persuade the laws that they are wrong, a feature not mentioned in the *Apology*. The whole thrust of the argument from the laws as parents is that a man must obey the laws, unless he can persuade them that they are wrong; in consequence, he could have an obligation to obey an unjust law. Socrates may not have intended that, but what he says commits him to it. We have, whether in interpreting Socrates or in thinking independently about obligation to obey the law, to keep distinct from each other three different claims, each of which can be found somewhere in what Socrates says:

1. A man must obey a law unless it is unjust.
2. A man must obey a law unless he believes that it is unjust.
3. A man must obey the law unless he persuades 'them' that it is unjust.

As to the third argument, that disobedience to the laws is destructive of the city, the claim made may be either conceptual or factual. But, whichever it is, if the claim is correct, then, as Wade concedes, it is correct whether or not the laws are just. If it is disobedience to law as such that is destructive of the city, and if a man must never do what is destructive of the city, then he must never disobey a law, no matter whether it is a just or unjust law. That argument provides no support whatever for the thesis that a man must not, or even need not, obey an unjust law (i.e. one by obeying which he performs or promotes injustice); and Socrates nowhere suggests that it does. We have to conclude that the conflict between, on the one hand, his principle that in no circumstances must a man do what is unjust or treat people badly and, on the other hand, his three arguments for obedience to the laws cannot be resolved, and that it can be papered over only by insufficient attention to the text.

A briefer but somewhat similar interpretation of the *Crito* has been advanced by Reginald Allen, who agrees with the view that Socrates' thesis does not require obedience to all law.[1] 'Since injury arises only from breach of authority and since authority extends only so far as agreement binds, to disobey a law or decree that enjoins the doing of injustice is not to injure the law.' But, first, Socrates says nothing whatever about authority extending only as far as agreement binds, and his first argument, from the laws as parents, makes it clear that he would deny that it did. And, secondly, whether or not disobedience to an unjust law injures the law (according to Socrates' second argument), it is certainly destructive of it (according to his third argument).

The reason why, says Allen, Socrates ought to accept the admittedly unjust verdict of his trial court and not avoid the consequentially unjust sentence is to be found in the nature of judicial authority. To deny the authority of a given sentence is to deny authority to any judicially rendered sentence; and that is to deny authority to law itself, for law cannot exist unless applied; and a city without law is not a city. If the destruction of the city is bad, which it is presumed to be, judicial decisions must be obeyed.

That is a fine defence of the need to abide by judicial decisions. But a closely similar argument could be constructed for the need to abide by legislative decisions; and if escape clauses are to be allowed for them, so that unjust laws will not be morally binding, it is by no means obvious why parity of reasoning would not allow the same or similar escape clauses from unjust judicial decisions.

Finally, we may well wonder why, if Socrates was maintaining that one should not obey actual laws which are unjust or which call for unjust conduct, he did not say so. The answer would appear to be that in the *Crito* it is real laws, or only such actual laws as are real laws, that he has in mind, and consequently that in that discussion the problem what a man should do when faced with an unjust law does not get serious

---

[1] R. E. Allen, 'Law and justice in Plato's *Crito*', 69 *Journal of Philosophy* (1972), pp. 562–6.

consideration. Persuasion as a permitted alternative to obedience, when it is justified as it is, viz. 'persuading her [one's country] in accordance with where justice really is' (51c), and 'persuade us, if there is something which we are not doing well' (51e), implies the possibility of laws being unjust; but Socrates shows no sign of thinking that the situation in which he finds himself calls for a discussion of them. We have to speculate what his solution would be, or rather what it would have to be to fit what he does say. If his νόμοι are real laws, then we have nothing to go on at all; if they are actual laws, then, if we are to start from his principle that in no circumstances must a man do what is unjust, some disobedience may be required; but, if we depend on his three arguments for obedience, then it is doubtful that disobedience should be allowed. The only way to avoid a conclusion with those ends loose is to pretend that in the text Socrates does not say some of the things that he does say.

CHAPTER FOUR

Duty to Obey the Laws as Parents

The first two arguments against the proposed disobedience to law are introduced by Socrates as *distinct* arguments: the first is an application of the principle that one should never treat anybody unjustly or badly even in retaliation for such treatment of oneself (49d); and the second ('the next point') is an application of the principle that a man must do whatever he agrees with another he will do, provided that what he agrees to is just (49e). Crito is invited to answer whether Socrates, if he were to leave Athens without permission, would be treating badly those whom he should least treat badly; and whether he would be keeping his just agreements (50a). When Crito replies that he does not know how to answer the questions, for he has not grasped them clearly, the device is brought in of introducing the laws themselves as speakers, who denounce the disobedience involved in the suggested gaol break as being destructive of law and of the city as a whole (50a–b). They thereupon develop each of the two arguments separately, yet strung together by the claim that Socrates' lawbreaking (if he goes ahead with it) will be destructive of law. Now, although it is not presented as such, that must be treated as a third and distinct line of argument. The argument presupposes that it is bad that laws be destroyed; for, without that presupposition, the fact (if it be one) that disobedience is destructive of law provides no kind of reason against disobedience. If lawbreaking is destructive of law, and if it is bad that laws be destroyed, then that is a good reason for its being wrong to disobey the law, irrespective of whether one has agreed to obey, irrespective even of whether what one has agreed to is just. Indeed, the weakness of the argument from destructiveness is that it requires us to suppose that law destruction is itself bad, and to make no discrimination between good and bad, possibly pernicious, laws. If some laws are better destroyed, and if they can be destroyed by disobedience to them, then disobedience to them could be shown to be wrong by the Destructiveness argument only if it could be shown that destroying them somehow involved, or had as its consequence, destructiveness to other parts of the system, or to the system as a whole, where those other parts of the system were better not destroyed.

Discussion of the Destructiveness argument will be taken up in Chapter Six, and of the Agreement argument in Chapter Five. The present chapter will concentrate on the first argument, viz. that for Socrates to break the law by escaping would be for him to treat badly those whom, least of all, he should treat badly. It runs 50a–51c, and it turns on the parental relationship of law to subject. When the laws claim to have begotten Socrates, to have brought him up, and to have educated him (50d, 51c), one is tempted to interpret it as a metaphor, as a way of expressing what is also said literally, viz. that it was under the marriage laws of Athens that he was the legitimate child of his actual parents, and that it was under the laws concerned with the rearing and education of children that he was brought up as he was, and that his father was required to get for him the education which he did. But, in light of the metaphysical view of the state later elaborated in the *Republic*, it could be that the talk here of laws as parents is less metaphorical than it might seem at first sight, that the state (in this passage not clearly distinguished from the laws) is the real parent of the subjects, with human parents as its agents. At any rate, it is seriously intended that, whatever is due from the individual to his human parents, exactly that, only even more so, is due from him to his fatherland. Those whom he will be treating badly by an illegal escape are those who, least of all, should be treated badly, viz. the laws of Athens which fathered him. He owes to the laws of his country all the duties which an offspring owes to his parents, and in particular the duty of obedience (subject only to the standing condition of being allowed to show where the path of justice lies, should it happen that the obedience called for does not accord with it).

The argument needs to be separated into two distinct strands, which are not in fact kept distinct throughout the passage. They may be called (1) the Filial Gratitude argument and (2) the Parental Authority argument. Each will be discussed in turn.

(1) The Filial Gratitude argument. This itself is a special form of the more general Benefits argument, according to which a reason (or, on a more uncompromising version, *the* reason) that it is wrong to break the law is that one is failing to discharge a social debt. The enjoyment of the benefits of living under the rule of law, such as some degree of personal security, some provision of institutional services, including education, and some rights in property, carries with it the obligation to submit oneself to the legal system which has made those benefits possible. We owe obedience as a fair price to pay for what we have received from the beneficent working of the legal system. And the argument will be that we owe the repayment for benefits by obedience not just to those laws from which we have directly benefitted (e.g. laws providing child support and education), but by obedience to the range of laws which make our society worth living in. The contribution of taxes for public funding of education is a fair price to pay, even for a childless couple, in return for all that they have received in other areas of their life by way of the stability and security which the legal system has given them.

In its pure form the Benefits argument has to be stated in the past tense (as it is so stated in the *Crito* version of it): obedience to law is owed as the duty in return for the benefits which have been received. When it is formulated in such a way as to include present and future benefits as well, it is liable to become entangled with the Agreement argument: that by continuing to accept the benefits of life under law one is agreeing to bear the costs of life under law, including the cost of obedience to laws which he would prefer not to obey. True, it can be formulated in a way which avoids that entanglement. It is essential to the obligation to keep to the terms of an agreement or contract that one in fact should be able to terminate or break it. In the case of benefits, the obligation (if it exists) of gratitude or repayment is always in respect of benefits so far received; and, for the future, the obligation will be at any time for benefits received until that time. One is able to break the obligation (simply by failing to discharge it, like failing to pay unpaid bills), but there is no way to terminate the obligation which he already has. What he may be able to do is to ensure that no further obligation is incurred, i.e. by receiving no further benefits. Whether he is able to ensure that will depend on whether he is able to avoid receiving the benefits; accepting benefits implies the ability to refuse them, receiving benefits does not.

The distinction between accepting and receiving becomes relevant to the parent-child relationship which Socrates sees as the human model of the law-subject relationship. Most of what a child gets from the love and care given by his parents cannot, without distortion, be described as what he has accepted from them, although all of it is what he has received from them. (In the *Laws* Plato goes still further, and describes the care and attention provided by parents to a child as a loan, the repayment of which he should regard as the first and greatest of his obligations, 717b–c.) Talk of acceptance becomes appropriate only at the stage of his development when, although he could somehow (however badly) manage on his own without what he gets from them, he does not. Now, what obligation of gratitude, i.e. of conduct in gratitude or repayment, does this impose on son or daughter towards parents? Some would want to say that, if the love and care which was freely given in upbringing and education was not freely accepted, then no obligation was incurred; the attempt which may be made to induce the offspring to feel obligation would be nothing but moral or emotional blackmail. On a strict interpretation of 'obligation' that may be true; but it should not be inferred that the son or daughter had no moral duty in return for what the parents had given. Simply in terms of benefit, the children of a normal family are better off for what their parents have done; furthermore, much of what the parents did would have been done over a period during which the children could not have done it for themselves; and they would have been lucky if, had their parents been unable to do it, substitute parents had done it half as well: at a minimum they were fed, clothed, housed, cared for when unwell, and taught—and all that with love. Without their parents they would have managed, either not at all or not as well, and they would not have had the love. So, anybody from a normal family who, on reaching adulthood, tried to draw up a balance sheet, would have to acknowledge how much he owed to his parents, including within that all that he received from them that he would have been helpless to secure for himself, and all that he had received from them which he could not be said to have accepted from them.

All this makes it plausible that children have certain duties to their parents, and that parents have certain rights against children—the more so when we attend to the contrary case, where unloving parents have done nothing for their children, have neglected them, or even have abandoned them. A child of such parents cannot be said to owe them anything, just because they have done nothing for him in return for which he might owe them duties of filial gratitude; the parents, on their side, by failing to care for the child, have forfeited whatever rights over him they might otherwise have held. If there is the analogy which (at least) Socrates claimed between parents-child and laws-subject, the subject's duty to obey and the laws' right to obedience will be subject to similar restriction.

Even as an analogy, let alone as a theory about the individual's relationship to the state or to the legal system, talk of laws as beneficent parents is unsatisfactory, because it ignores the points of disanalogy. The only duty which the subject has to the laws is that which Socrates is concerned to stress, viz. that of obedience, or, more accurately, that of not breaking the law. The law can demand no more of a man than that his conduct be not in fact in violation of it. But such conduct will not have been performed in obedience to the law, unless the fact that that is what the law requires forms some part of the explanation of the conduct being what it is. The law requires certain acts and forbearances, not those acts and forbearances out of obedience to the law; if they are done out of obedience, that may be a socially healthy bonus, but it is a bonus. On the other hand, during that period of their lives when people owe obedience to their parents, it is obedience that they owe, not merely conduct of a sort which in fact accords with parental requirements. Obeying and disobeying alike must be knowingly done, behaving in accordance with the law and breaking it alike need not be. In the *Crito* the distinction is blurred by representing laws, in an Austinian way, as commands of the system (e.g. twice in 50b), but with the emphasis on situations of the military type, where the commands are typically (and not in an Austinian way) particular, so that responding conduct can hardly fail to be either obedient or disobedient.

If, however, we use 'obedience' in the looser sense, so that conduct that is in accordance with law is in obedience to it (even if not performed out of obedience to it), then we may return to the point that that is the one duty which the subject has to the laws, and which, moreover, he has as a continuing duty, at least as long as he has been enjoying the benefits of the law. But, in the case of his parents, not only does he normally have other duties besides, but that particular one is just the one which lapses when he reaches maturity. The one right which the legal system may be said to have against the subject is one which abides; for parents it is only one among others, and it is the very one which does not abide.

Again, the idea that duty of obedience is owed for the benefits and advantages which one has enjoyed is more appropriate to the case of laws than to that of parents. In both cases benefits will have been received, without which the individual would have been much worse off, and which he could not have provided for himself. But what is owed in return, and the reason why it is owed, are different in each of the two cases. The so-called duty of a child to obey its parents falls within the period when it is inappropriate to speak of a child as having moral duties at all, i.e. the period before he has acquired the concept of duty. And the duties which he may later have towards the parents in return for what they earlier did for him will be, not duties of obedience, but duties of family affection, respect, and response to the needs of the parents if a time comes when they find themselves in a position something like that in which their child once was, viz. that of being unable without help to provide for their own needs. In the case of the law the duty owed is that of obedience (at least in the looser sense), and for a quite different, more general and more impersonal reason. The benefits we receive from living under a system of law are not just those which we receive from those laws in the system which work directly to our advantage (e.g. tax relief to home-owners for the interest element in their mortgage; this provides a relief only to those individuals who are buying property on mort-gage); they are also those which we indirectly receive from having others both meeting their legal requirements (e.g. pay-

ing their taxes) and living peaceably because of the direct
advantages which they get from such laws as do directly benefit
them. The subject's relationship to the law is therefore much
more complex than an offspring's relationship to his parents;
what the law has done for him includes some of what it has
done for others, and how their conduct has matched up to it.

The kind of feeling which it is natural for a person to have for
his parents it is hard to have towards laws, especially under
modern conditions where they usually impinge on the subject's
consciousness only when they frustrate him, fail to give him
what he thinks they should, or bewilder him by their obscurity.
For the rest, he takes them for granted, and would not understand being invited to regard the legal system as he regards his
parents. Socrates makes the psychological obstacle lower by
having the laws in this passage identify themselves with his
πόλις and his πατρίς. Most people would be less embarrassed to
be asked to love their country than to be asked to love their
laws. But such a move, emotionally telling although it may be,
is intellectually disreputable. Socrates was not a 'my country,
right or wrong' man, and would have been ashamed of some of
his country's conduct during the Peloponnesian War, e.g. the
Melian massacre. For Americans the long-drawn-out trauma
of their war in Vietnam has been only partly finding themselves
for the first time on the losing side, much more the experience
of their country being led by the executive power of their
President deeper and deeper into a morass of illegality and
immorality. The ties of filial and patriotic loyalty can be
admirable, but Socrates could not have approved of their being
treated as morally the strongest ties.

The use made of the laws-as-parents figure is to emphasise
that between law and subject, as between parent and child, the
relation of justice is not one of symmetrical equality; whatever
treatment the law gives to the subject, believing it to be just,
will not necessarily be just for the subject to give to the law
(50e). Just as a son is not free to talk back or hit back at his
father, when scolded or beaten by him, so the subject is not
free to destroy laws or country in retaliation for the laws
destroying him.

Apart from its role in the development of the argument for
obedience to law, this passage is interesting for what it appears

to assert about rights, that parents have rights against their
children which the latter do not have against them, and indeed
that such parental rights are dual, the positive right to treat
certain individuals (their children) in various ways, and the
negative right not themselves to be so treated by them. On the
other hand, it has been suggested that a concept of rights is
quite alien to Greek thought of the time, and that an indication
of that is that Greek contains no word for 'rights'.[1] It is true
that there is none, and that its absence gives a reason for supposing at least that a concept of rights, if there at all, was little
developed and not of central interest. But the absence of a word
is not conclusive evidence of the non-existence of a concept.
The facts that Aristotle characterised the popular notion of
justice in terms of 'having one's own' (τὰ αὑτῶν ἕκαστοι ἔχουσι,
Rhet. 1336b9–10), and that Plato held that the aim of lawcourts
trying private actions was to see to it that people neither held
what belonged to others nor were deprived of their own, on the
ground that such an outcome was just (*Rep.* 433e), suggest that
by the time of Socrates some at least rudimentary concept of
rights may have been held. Furthermore, Hart's claim that a
moral code could exist containing the notion of duties but not
that of rights seems contestable. If A owes a duty to B, then
there is a way in which B can claim its performance or com-
plain about its non-performance, but in which a third party C
cannot: B, in making his complaint, would have a standing
which C would not have. Again, while there was nothing in
Attic law closely resembling the modern notion of a legal right,
as in property law, and while it is not clear that there was a
distinction between ownership and possession, there certainly
was property law, which is absolutely unintelligible without
some notion of legal right or entitlement. Private ownership is
often mentioned by Homer in the *Odyssey* (e.g., 2. 78, 203,
14. 92, 18. 144). The distinction between possession/ownership
and use (κτῆσις and χρῆσις) was familiar, and is reflected in
Plato's figure of the aviary at *Theaet.* 197b–c, where he con-
trasts the κτῆσις and the ἕξις of knowledge: to know is to pos-
sess knowledge as a man possesses a coat which he has bought

---

[1] Cf. H. L. A. Hart, 'Are there any natural rights?', in A. M. Quinton
(ed.), *Political Philosophy* (Oxford: Oxford University Press, 1967), p. 54.

F

but is not at present wearing, or possesses the birds which he has in a cage; that is to be contrasted with the use of knowledge, like wearing the coat or holding one of the birds in his hands. There were various legal remedies, such as action by an owner of land against his exclusion from it by the occupant, and action to establish title. There was the right of a citizen to his freedman's services for a given period after manumission. There was ἀτιμία, the deprivation of legal rights; and so on. The argument against suicide in the *Phaedo* is that a human being is the property (κτήματα) of the gods, and therefore may not kill himself unless required by a god to do so (62b–c). And finally, in the *Crito* itself, the use, already mentioned, of the transitive verbs ἀδικεῖν and κακῶς ποιεῖν suggests a more personal view of justice than the view later developed in the *Republic*. There, to act unjustly is to step outside one's role, to presume to usurp another's role, where that is inappropriate to one's social skill or assignment; but there is no indication there that the act does an injustice *to* the other person, that he is the victim of injustice. But, consistently throughout the *Crito* that is where the emphasis lies: one must never do injustice *to* another, even in return for injustice received from him; and, in particular, Socrates must not treat the laws unjustly, as he would if he were to allow the gaol break to be executed. We cannot say that the notion of a right, whether legal or moral, had leapt fully formed from the head of Zeus, but we can hardly deny that there was enough there to make it appropriate to talk of it in terms of rights.

(2) The Parental Authority argument. The argument that laws, like parents, are owed obedience in return for the benefits they have conferred on those subject to them merges in 50e into the argument that laws, like parents *and masters*, are owed obedience because of their *authority* relationship to the subjects. The transition can be found, although it is not stressed, in the final recapitulatory sentence of the Filial Gratitude argument: 'Since you were both born and brought up and educated, could you deny, first, that you were ours, our child and *our servant*?' (50e1–3; my italics). Being a servant is no part of being a son owing obedience to a father who has discharged his duty of providing upbringing and education, but it is a way, a different way, of being subject to an authority; and that is the

way which is developed through the remainder of this passage. It is not claimed that laws, parents or masters have the right to treat subjects, children or servants in any way at all that they please. That would amount to the claim that a government required no further justification for any piece of lawmaking than that it was an expression of its will. What is claimed is that, if it expresses its will in a way which it believes to be just, even though that may be to the disadvantage or injury of a subject, the subject has no right to treat it in the same way in return, and has a duty not to. The government does have a right to treat subjects in a way which it believes to be just, and it does have a positive right to their compliance, together with the negative right to their not treating it in the same way. It may be all right for government or laws to destroy subject, but it cannot be all right for subject to destroy government or laws.

The idea that the state has a right to obedience, just because it is the state and we are its members or subjects, is more congenial to the kind of enlightened authoritarianism which Plato presented in the *Republic* than it is to modern liberalism; and it may have accorded with the feelings of patriotism which Socrates had for Athens. But the parental model of laws is suitable only to a highly paternalistic society, one in which people are considered as having interests, but not rights, at least not rights that are not conferred on them by legal action of the state. It is suitable to the *Republic*, where it is hard to discover even a hint of an individual having rights; the talk there is all of the duties of justice, not of its rights. But it is less suitable to the Socrates of the *Apology*, who both in the imagined story of his discharge (29d) and in the episode of Leon of Salamis (32c–d) was committing himself to the view that one could have not only a right but a duty to disobey. The *Apology* view allows the individual a freedom which the *Crito* view and the *Republic* view do not. The passage in the *Crito* does allow the limited freedom of persuading (or trying to persuade) authority to change its mind before submitting to it, while the *Republic* allows none. At least, it allows none in the case of justice, although arguably it allows some in the case of temperance: the doctrine there is not just that of my station and its duties, but also that of accepting my station as being my proper station (431d–e).

The parent/master model of the state (laws) is disturbing, not only because it minimises or even denies individual rights against it, but also because its own right to obedience to its will is extralegal. Not that there is anything wrong with there being extralegal rights. But to allow that the state's right to obedience from its subjects is such is to concede to the state a metaphysical status which belongs to myth rather than to reason. Although we have by now attained some immunity from the myth, many still believe, and if political leaders and police chiefs had their way all of us would believe, that a powerful reason (possibly the principal, if not the only, reason) that we should obey a law is that it is a law. In fact, with the exception of a special class of laws, it is no reason at all. If the conduct prescribed by a law is morally or socially desirable (e.g. refraining from murder, violence, deceit, etc.), reason for obeying the law is provided by the desirability of the conduct; justification of the conduct is its desirability, not its conformity to law. There are good reasons for having it prescribed and, so far as possible, policed by law, but they are distinct from whatever reason there is for the prescribed conduct. And if, due to change in circumstances or attitudes, the conduct ceases to be desirable, no reason persists for continuing to obey *that* law. That there is a law requiring certain conduct can provide no good reason for obeying it, if the justification for the law lies in the desirability of the conduct, and if the conduct is in fact not, or no longer, desirable. There may still be good reasons for obeying such a law, when it no longer serves a valuable social purpose, but they will have to be reasons other than that it is a law prescribing the conduct which it does. Again, there is nothing about the law's being a law which grounds, even *prima facie* grounds, an obligation to obey it, as there is, say, about a promise's being a promise which *prima facie* grounds an obligation to keep it. If there is an initial presumption in favour of obedience to such a law, it is because of something, not about it itself, but about the legal system to which it belongs. Similar considerations apply to what may be called uniformity law, where the direct thrust of the law is to the method of attaining a purpose, rather than to the purpose itself, and where it is indifferent which of several effective methods is chosen, provided only that whatever method is chosen is uniformly adhered to. Traffic laws are a familiar instance. It does not matter whether traffic in a given area keeps to the right or keeps to the left, whether traffic coming in from the right does or does not have priority, whether a turn to the left (or to the right, as the case may be) is or is not permitted on a red light. But it does matter that there should be one uniform rule for the area. Whatever there is to be said for such a law is whatever there is to be said for the practice which the law requires; and the reason for acting in accordance with the law, or for conforming one's conduct to it, lies in the value of the practice. The practice derives none of its value from the law, and that that is the law provides no reason for conformity, although it indicates that there is a reason and what it is.

The special class of laws which provides an exception consists of those laws which both constitute and police activities and institutions which are created by law, and which could not exist at all in the absence of appropriate laws. While it is possible to kill intentionally or to refrain from it, to drive one's car to the danger or not to the danger of the public, even in the absence of homicide and traffic laws, it is not possible to participate in the electoral process, and to conduct oneself either properly or improperly, whether as voter or as electoral official, in the absence of appropriate electoral law. In such cases 'because it is the law' can be a good reason for conduct, because the conduct could not bear the description which it does in the absence of law. The 'because it is the law' principle is a long way after the 'because the law has a right to obedience' principle of the *Crito*, but it is a descendant of it, and the earlier principle, even if we discount the metaphysical claims embodied in it, has the same defects as the later principle.

Something remains to be said about the Benefits argument for obedience to law, of which the *Crito*'s Filial Gratitude argument is a special form: if the duty to obey the law is tied to the benefits received from the law, it has to be remembered that such benefits, and consequently the duty, are both contingent and variable. The first claim which the personified laws of Athens made on Socrates' obedience (50d) was based on a very small class of laws, viz. those concerned with his parenthood and upbringing, just those laws which affected him through the medium of his human parents. And the claim was based on the supposed fact that the operation of those laws was in his case beneficial. That Socrates is asked whether he has any fault to find with their operation implies that such laws could fail to benefit, and consequently that *this* reason for his having a duty to obey could fail. It should not be forgotten that the benefits of living under particular laws, or under a particular system of laws, or under a system of law at all are not necessary consequences of such living, and vary enormously from one individual to another with differences in social and economic conditions. Unhappily, the youths most often picked on by judges, at the time of sentencing, for moral homilies about having to pay their debt to society are the very ones who can most appropriately ask what society has ever done for them. It is not that society owes them a living. But, if society is going to punish them for breaking laws which they find it inconvenient or disagreeable to keep, and is going to justify the punishment as enforced payment of the dues of gratitude for benefits received, then the empirical question whether, and how extensively, benefits have been provided, i.e. have actually got through to the offenders themselves, should not be ignored. There may be, even so, other reasons why such offenders should be punished, but to tell a young junkie caught robbing a grocery store that he must be made, by being sent to gaol, to pay his debt to society can be insensitive to the point of hypocrisy.

If the stronger version of the Benefits argument is advanced, to the effect that *the* reason why we should obey lies in the benefits we have received, then it is implausible to present the argument in terms of individual laws or categories of law. For that would mean that we had a duty to obey only *those* laws from the operation of which we had benefitted. It would be better to say that we had a duty to obey those individual laws as parts of a system of law from which as a whole we had benefitted. Even that would be inadequate without some supplementation. For, if a particular law is not beneficial to me, how does the fact by itself that it belongs to a system of law which on the whole or otherwise is beneficial to me provide a reason that I ought to obey it? Some further factor needs to be brought in, if the argument from benefit is to work in the case of a non-benefitting law belonging to an otherwise beneficial body of laws. Such a factor might be the one which Socrates adduces: the bad consequences for the system of disobedience by one of its members; or again it might be the unfairness to others of not sharing the burden of inconvenient obedience. A supplementary factor of the first kind would keep the argument within the scope of benefits: it would be the argument that disobedience to an admittedly non-benefitting law would diminish, even ultimately destroy, the benefits of the system as a whole; whether such an argument is valid remains yet to be discussed. A factor of the second kind would take the argument outside the scope of benefits. It may indeed be the case that a contingent but common consequence of treating others unfairly will be that they will act unfairly too, and that the benefits which accrue from a system of fair reciprocity will diminish or be lost. But to treat that as the reason for treating them fairly is to devalue the currency of fairness.

Finally, if there is a law from which most have not benefitted, although it is part of a system of law from which most have benefitted, is it clearly wrong to disobey that law? It may be an ill-conceived law prohibiting an activity which is better left to individual judgment, e.g. the law still surviving in some penal codes making unmarried cohabitation a criminal offence. It may be a law prohibiting or restricting free exchange of ideas in printed or other publications. A good deal more than simple membership of a beneficial system of law is needed before an argument of the Benefits kind can tell in favour of a law and against an individual, whom the operation of that law does not benefit.

CHAPTER FIVE

Contractual Duty to Obey the Laws

The argument for obligation to keep the laws based on an agreement to keep them has never been stated more simply, briefly and concisely than it is by Plato in the *Crito*. It occupies less than two pages (51c–53a), it is displayed with a clarity that has not been surpassed by any of the later and better-known versions of the social contract theory, and it sets out the theory in the only way in which it could have any hope of being tenable. The standard objection to the theory, that it rests on bad, because unevidenced, history in supposing a precontractual state of nature, and the standard reply to that objection, that the theory does not rest on history at all, let alone bad history, but is an analysis of the conditions logically presupposed by the facts of political allegiance—both alike miss the point, which is that, if the theory is to be tenable at all, it must be based on history, but the history must be the history of the present. What happened in the past, recent and remote alike, *is* irrelevant, because it cannot provide the ground for an individual *now* having an obligation to obey his government or its laws. What any of those before him may have agreed to do does not matter, for, although it may have bound them, it cannot bind him. For the same reason that failure to discover a contract in the past cannot harm the theory success in discovering one would not help it. More often than is supposed one can be discovered, not by delving back into the remote past and finding evidence of a pre-political or pre-social state of nature followed by a meeting and an agreement emerging from it, but by finding agreements which have changed an existing society from one form into another. The American revolution is, perhaps, a simple example of such a change; but the constitutional duties of present-day Americans are not accounted for by their being the lineal heirs (the few of them that are) to the events of 1779. And for the vast majority of American citizens, most of whom have become citizens, either directly or indirectly, by immigration, whatever obligation they have to obey the laws of the new country to which their fathers came does not derive from any oath of allegiance which their fathers gave; the only oath of allegiance which can morally bind a man, whether he be immigrant, enrolling soldier, novitiate priest or whatever, is the oath of allegiance which he gives himself. But he must *give* one; and that is why the standard answer on behalf of the social contract theory is as bad as the standard objection which it is intended to answer. If he has not himself given allegiance, then either he owes none or there must be some other explanation of his owing it. If he has not agreed to conduct himself in a certain way, then, if he does have an obligation to conduct himself that way, it is simply false that he has it *because* he agreed to it; his obligation cannot rest on an agreement which was not given by him, either because it was given by somebody else (such as his father or forefathers) or because it was given by nobody at all.

The problem for contract theory is to decide what is to count as giving agreement, and what is the status and force of the obligation so generated; the laws, in their address to Socrates, have plenty to say about the first, nothing about the second. Again, they do not raise the question whether distinctions can usefully be drawn, first between an agreement and a valid agreement, and secondly between an agreement's being valid and its being one which the party has a binding obligation to keep.

Beginning in 51c, the laws very succinctly state the case for contractual obligation to obey the law. By Athenian law any citizen was free to leave the city by emigration any time that he pleased, whether to move to one of its colonies, if he was not satisfied with the laws or the way things were managed at home, or to go anywhere abroad that he wanted—and there were no restrictions on his going: he could take all his belongings with him. By enacting this liberty the laws publicly declared to any Athenian that if, on attaining his majority, he did not like the laws and management of the city, he was free to go wherever he liked, taking what was his with him. And it was not a once-in-a-lifetime liberty, which a person had to exercise, if he was ever going to exercise it at all, *at* the time at which he officially attained manhood. That might seem to be what is suggested by the mention in 51d3, when coupled with the point next made (51e), that anyone who stays in the city is deemed thereby to have agreed to do whatever the laws order him to do. The two passages might easily be taken together to mean that, in a person's life, there is just one time at which he is free to go, such that, if he does not, then at that time he has agreed to obey the laws; and thereafter he would not be free—he would be 'bound by the contract'. But that is not what is meant: Socrates is later reminded that the decision whether to go or to stay is not one which he had to take in a hurry—he had had seventy years during which he was free to go if he were not satisfied with the laws (52e); and even as recently as his trial he could have chosen banishment as his sentence if he had wanted to (52c). The picture is indeed of an agreement made at a definite time, that of officially reaching manhood, but an agreement which was being continuously renewed by continued domicile in the city, or one which could be terminated by the individual at any time that he saw fit subsequent to having made it. One of the conditions allowed under which he had been free to go any time during his seventy years was '. . . if the agreements appeared to you to be unjust'. So, he had been free to go at any time that either he was dissatisfied with the laws or found his agreement to abide by them was unjust; the agreement had to be a thing past, on which he could look back and find it just or unjust, as the case might be.

The claim that the agreement was not got out of Socrates by coercion, or by deceit or by allowing him insufficient time to think (52e) assimilates it to modern law, and to the protection given to a purchaser of goods under a hire purchase agreement. In English law under the Theft Act 1968 ss. 15–16 obtaining property or pecuniary advantage by deception is a criminal offence; under the law of contract a contract obtained by duress or misrepresentation is voidable; and under the Consumer Credit Act 1974 ss. 67–68 a person who signs a consumer credit agreement has the right in certain circumstances to cancel the agreement within a fixed cooling-off period. To protect, e.g., gullible housewives from the guiles of fast-talking door-salesmen, by giving them a chance to reflect on the financial consequences of an agreement which they have been talked into signing for, say, taking out magazine subscriptions or purchasing encyclopaedias on instalments, and allowing them to change their minds before they are finally committed, the law provides a cooling-off period of a certain number of hours between the signing of an agreement and its coming into effect. The modern growth of deficit buying and its extension to the individual purchaser who, in most cases, is far less experienced and far less capable than the buying officers of a public corporation of appreciating what he is letting himself in for, has made it necessary to temper the severity of *caveat emptor*. The principle is exactly the one appealed to by the laws in reminding Socrates that he has had all the time he needed for making up his mind whether the agreement which he had given to obey them had been just.

So the argument is quite simply that Socrates had agreed to obey the law, the agreement had been given under fair conditions, and he had all the time in the world to change his mind, if he had wanted to. The conclusion from the premises that he had agreed under conditions that were fair, and that he had not exercised his right to dissolve the agreement by departing, viz. that he had the obligation to obey the laws, is never actually stated, but is clearly accepted as following, and as required by the principle already enunciated by Socrates himself (49e, 50a), that a man must stand by his agreements provided that they are just, and by the reproach imagined levelled by the laws at Socrates, for considering that he might be justified in escaping on the ground that he had been unjustly treated by the city in being wrongly convicted: '. . . or did you agree to abide by whatever court decisions the city pronounces?' (50c). The laws take it as so clear as not to need stating that a man must do what he has agreed to do (with no explicit mention made of Socrates' earlier provision that what he has agreed to do itself be just). The questions whether, and why, a man who has made an agreement ought to abide by it, and whether, if he has such an obligation, it might conceivably be overriden, are nowhere discussed, although in any treatment making pretensions to completeness they should be. The presupposition throughout the two pages of this argument is that the obligation to obey the laws engendered by an agreement to obey them is an absolute obligation, as indeed it was in Socrates' original formulation: it is something that *must* be done (ποιητέον, 49e6), and the man who does not do it will be doing what is wrong (51e); there is no question here of *prima facie* obligations, or of the possibility of conflicting obligations. As the beginning of the story of the obligation to abide by agreements it may do, but as the end of the story it would not.

Not only were the laws right in presenting Socrates' contractual obligation of obedience as self-imposed, but they were also right in bringing out that there is more than one way of agreeing, and that a man cannot deny that he has agreed merely because he has not *said* that he agreed; conduct other than performatory declarations can count as agreements, or expressions of agreement.[1] The most straightforward ways of agreeing to do something, as of promising, of accepting an offer, etc., are ways that consist of saying, in speech or writing, that one agrees to do it, e.g., by in the appropriate circumstances, and with the appropriate conditions fulfilled, orally agreeing (using the spoken words 'I agree to . . .', or their equivalent), or by signing a written agreement. But any conduct at all that is mutually understood to constitute by convention an expression of agreement does constitute such an expression. What the convention will be depends upon factors such as the context and the group to which the participants belong: it could be shaking hands on a bargain, a nod of the head, spitting on the ground, putting one's money on the table, etc. By none of these performances would a man be *saying* that he agreed, but he would be *as good as* saying that he agreed, if it were conventionally understood that such a performance expressed an agreement. And the laws' point to Socrates is that it does not matter whether a

---

[1] Throughout this chapter I use 'expression' and 'express' as communication words, i.e. to mean that what is being expressed is being expressed *to* somebody. This applies both in the instance of expressing agreement, which is an essential element of the chapter's topic of discussion, and also in the illustration of expressing a desire (p. 102). In another context a distinction might need to be drawn between simply expressing a desire and expressing a desire to someone. But, as the first plays no part in the chapter, the phrase 'expressing a desire' is used as an abbreviation for 'expressing a desire to someone'. I do not, that is, wish to deny that 'express' can properly be used in a non-communicating sense; but it is only in its communicating sense that it is used here.

citizen has explicitly said that he agreed to abide by the law; there may be, indeed there is, conduct which counts as agreeing; so his agreement to be obedient to the laws of Athens is indicated by what he *does* (ὡμολογηκέναι ἔργῳ, 51e3). Specifically, his remaining in Athens, when, after reaching official manhood, he is free to leave without any loss of goods or property, either implies or expresses (the laws do not make the distinction) his agreement to obey the laws of Athens. The latter is the doctrine later especially associated with John Locke, and through him commonly known as tacit agreement or consent. The idea is that, by not taking advantage of the liberty which he has to leave the jurisdiction in which he finds himself, a man shows himself to be satisfied with the laws to which he is subject and with the way the city is run, and expresses his agreement, not by his words, but by his conduct (ἔργῳ ἀλλ᾽ οὐ λόγῳ, 52d5), i.e. by staying, to live *as* a citizen. Living as, or playing one's part as, a citizen includes keeping to one's agreements, and is to be contrasted with what is to be expected from the meanest type of slave, who will try to run away contrary to agreements and undertakings given (52d). And the notion that the man who stays, although he is at full liberty to leave, provides clear proof of his satisfaction with the way things are done in his city, and that he agrees to obey, applies, Socrates concedes, especially to himself, because he has spent an exceptionally large portion of his life inside Athens: he has, with one exception, never left the city to attend a festival or games, he has never been anywhere else except on military service, he has never travelled outside as other people do, and he has never shown any inclination to see for himself other cities and other systems of law (52b); if ever a man chose to live in his own city and agreed to play his part as a citizen of it, it was Socrates.

The idea that a man who is free to leave his country should either leave it or, if he stays, obey its laws is a common enough one, and was well caught by the bumper sticker frequently seen in the U.S.A. during the Vietnam war, 'America—Love It Or Leave It'. It may be an acceptable idea, but it does not indicate the reason, or even that there is a reason, that it should be accepted. It should, therefore, be distinguished, as it not always is, from either the doctrine of implied agreement or that of tacit agreement. It is not true that, merely by staying when he is free to go, a man either implies his agreement or silently expresses his agreement to obey. It is possible to stay, although free to go, and yet not to have agreed to obey. For one thing, he might not know that he was free to go, when in fact he was. He might believe that he was not free, and in that case his staying could not be interpreted as implying or expressing any agreement on his part. Even if he knew or believed that he was free to go, his staying could not by itself properly be interpreted as implying or expressing an agreement. He might stay simply because he wanted to, because it suited him to stay, because he could not think of anywhere else that he could go to and would prefer to be; and he might let it be known that he did not wish his staying to be construed as either implying or expressing an agreement to obey the laws; in that case his staying would not either imply or express his agreement. It might still be true that his staying did impose on him an obligation to obey the laws, but the reason that it did, e.g. that it was unfair to others that he should gain the advantages from their obeying the laws, without making a proportionate contribution himself, might not involve an agreement. When we are told that the man who stays, when he is free to go, by staying imposes on himself the obligation of obedience, we are not being offered any reason for the obligation; we are not being told why it is true that, when he stays, he imposes an obligation on himself. In the other two cases we are: we are told that he ought to obey because his staying implies an agreement to obey, or because by staying he expresses an agreement to obey. We do not yet have to concede that they are good reasons, but they are being offered to us *as* good reasons. In the case which is to be described merely as staying, although free to go, we are not yet being offered anything as a good reason for obedience.

If merely staying, when free to leave, does not by itself imply agreement, what more is needed for the implication? The laws tell Socrates that they have substantial and positive proof (μεγάλα τεκμήρια, 52b1) that he is pleased with the city and its laws—his almost unbroken residence there and his disinclination even to visit other places. It should be noted that it is said that his continuous residence in the city shows his satisfaction, not that by his continuous residence he shows his satisfaction. The latter would be claiming that by behaving as he had Socrates expressed his satisfaction (or, possibly, that from his behaviour he wanted the agreement to be inferred), the former makes the different claim that from his behaviour his satisfaction can be inferred. Can it? Does a man's continuing in a situation, when he is free, and when it is known to himself and to everyone else that he is free, to move himself from it, imply that he is pleased or satisfied with the way things are run and with the laws to which he is subject in that situation? It may be some evidence that he is, but it is far from amounting to positive proof or implication. It does imply satisfaction, in a minimal sense, with the situation itself—that he is unaware of a situation anywhere else which he thinks would be preferable, or which he prefers sufficiently to overcome the inertia of continuing with his familiar way of life in its familiar surroundings. He may think it a pretty poor way of life, wish it were better, and be able to think of ways in which it would be better, without having a strong enough drive or enough energy to uproot himself. So, he is satisfied with the situation in the bare sense that he is resigned to it, prepared to put up with it rather than make the effort necessary for change; but he is not on that account satisfied with the situation, in the sense of being pleased with it, or being glad to be in it, or feeling satisfaction in it. And, even if he were in the stronger sense satisfied with his situation, it would not follow that he was in that sense satisfied with his state's way of government or laws. If a man (1) has to choose between staying in one place, with its government and its laws, and moving to another place, with *its* government and *its* laws, and (2) does choose to stay where he is, and (3) is pleased or satisfied with the situation in which he finds himself in the place where he is, it cannot with any certainty be inferred that he is pleased or satisfied with that place's government or laws. Whether or not he is will depend on further factors, such as the extent to which and the manner in which the government and its laws impinge on his life. If he were economically or culturally fairly self-sufficient, they might impinge very little. Or they might impinge on him as much as they do on most of us, and he might not like them at all, but even so prefer to stay where he was because of the other advantages of his present situation. In that case, he would choose to stay where he was, and be pleased on the whole with his situation, despite not being pleased with the government and the laws. All that can be inferred from his staying, when there is somewhere else to which it is known that he can go, is that he prefers the total present situation which includes government and laws to the total situation in the other place which includes its government and its laws. It cannot be inferred that the government and laws are themselves a preferred part of the total preferred situation. And even the preference for the total situation may be a negative one, that he has not preferred the situation, or prospect of it, in another place—if he had, he would have moved. His preference for the present situation may amount to no more than his not having seriously considered, or even contemplated at all, an alternative which he knew to exist. The fact that in seventy years Socrates had hardly set foot outside Athens, except when serving in the army, may be a reflection of his love of Athens or it may be a reflection of his temperament and personality; but it tells us very little that is reliable of his regard for the city's government and political institutions, or for its laws.

But, even though staying when free to go does not imply satisfaction with government and laws, it might imply agreement to obey them; it might even express agreement to obey them. Those two possibilities have to be considered, not only because they are left open by the rejection of the claim that staying implies satisfaction with government and laws, but also because they are closer to the heart of the *Crito* argument. Even if a man is not pleased with his government and the laws, he may still have agreed to obey them, and he may have a consequential obligation to obey them. In a parliamentary election one may strongly support one party and oppose the other, yet accept the outcome of the election when it goes against him, and agree to be ruled by the other and successful party's government, which he dislikes and disapproves of; that is the fundamental political principle of parliamentary democracy. And, on the other hand, a man may approve of government and laws, have an obligation to obey them, and yet not have that obligation deriving from an agreement. In a modern state, although there may be some who have a contractual obligation to obey the law, there are very many who do not. But it is impossible to claim, on that account alone, that they have no obligation at all to obedience; and for those who actually do have it their obligation will have to be other than contractual.

So, whatever the answer to the question whether his continued residence in the city gave positive proof of his satisfaction with its way of government and its laws, the question still remains whether Socrates, by staying when he was free to go, and to go without suffering economic loss, agreed to obey the laws. And that question is, as has been indicated (although not yet explained), ambiguous: it may be a question about implied agreement, or it may be a question about tacit agreement. Each has to be considered. If a man has an obligation, or if, more strongly, he has an absolute obligation to keep his agreements (possibly with the exception of those that are not just), then it is important to determine whether a man in Socrates' position *has* agreed to obey the law. That he has agreed is the whole case against Socrates, the would-be escaper, at this point.

Implied agreement and tacit agreement are easily distinguished but often confused. Tacit agreement is a way of agreeing; implied or implicit agreement is not. Tacit agreement is any way there is of agreeing, or expressing agreement, silently, i.e. without words spoken or written. Implying agreement is not a way of agreeing, but a way, any way that there is, of implying that there already is agreement, that one *has* agreed; whether an agreement, which is implied, must have been explicit, verbally or tacitly, is a question. If we ask whether Socrates' conduct, i.e. remaining in Athens when he was free to go, implied that he had undertaken to obey its laws, we are asking whether from the fact of his so staying we may infer that he had undertaken to obey. In general, in voluntarily entering a rule-governed activity (a game of tennis, or golf, or bridge would be simple instances), one accepts the rules, commits oneself to playing according to them; that is a generally understood convention (in a Humean sense)— not that any agreeing has been going on, but that there is an agreement in the way which lawyers have called 'a meeting of the minds'. Anybody who, playing in an unrefereed game of tennis, deliberately tried to gain an advantage by serving with his foot across the baseline, and who met his opponent's protest with the retort that he knew that it was against the rules, but that he had not, before

G

starting to play, been asked to agree, nor had he spontaneously agreed, to play according to the rules of tennis, would rightly be regarded as a barrack-room lawyer, not to be played with again. By playing tennis together, and most clearly in the unrefereed games which most games of tennis are, people do imply their agreement to play according to the rules. It is not that there is any tacit agreement before beginning to play on the particular occasion, or before beginning to play in the first place, but that each player understands that the other expects that the game will be played by each of them according to the rules, and that neither does anything beforehand to disabuse the other of his understanding. That can be said to amount to an agreement, although nothing has been done which can be said to amount to a tacit agreement, for there has been no conduct by either party which symbolically *expresses* his agreement. A game, because it is a wholly rule-constituted and rule-governed activity, such that conduct within it has its point wholly determined by the rules, provides a particularly clear example of the convention that participants undertake to be, and understand themselves to be, bound by the rules. A player does not owe his opponent an explicit agreement, tacit or otherwise, to keep to the rules; he would owe him a disclaimer, if there was a rule, or there were rules, which he intended not to keep. Sometimes in a friendly game, owing to local or weather conditions, one of the rules may seem better modified or suspended for the occasion; the implied agreement requires that *that* change be explicitly agreed between the players.

Now, although in many respects the playing of games is an illuminating model for living in society under law, it is a long way from being a perfect paradigm; and the dissimilarities are important. The two chief differences relevant to the present subject stem from the 'contracting in' character of playing games, and from the fact that it is wholly constituted by rules. To take the latter first. Because a game is wholly rule-constituted, it is impossible to describe how that game is played except in terms of the rules. An Englishman's description of cricket for a bewildered American, or an American's description of football for a confused Englishman, however crude and watered down it may be to suit the other's ignorance, is basically a paraphrase of the rules of the game, i.e. an account of the activities of the players which *has* to be given in the categories and concepts of the game; any account that was not simply would not *be* an account of that game, and, if it were not given in the framework of some rule-concepts and categories or other, would not be an account of any game at all. Remove mention of defining rules, liberty rules, prohibitory rules and penalty rules from the description of how a game of cricket, football, chess or whatever is played, and there would be no description left. Picking up how a particular game is played is picking up, however inarticulately, what its rules are; and it would be impossible to play in a game without awareness that it had rules, and without some awareness, however dim, what at least the central rules were. That is broadly true, although there is considerable variation of complexity and sophistication from one game to another: it is possible for small children to play soccer of a sort, knowing little more about it than that it is a game in which you kick a ball in the direction of your opponents' goal and run after it with the aim of kicking it through; on the other hand there is no playing chess at all without some grasp of the allowed, prohibited and required moves of the various pieces.

Living in political society, whether Athens of the fifth/fourth century B.C. or a modern nation-state, is a different business. There will be rules of both kinds (constitutive and regulative), but the constitutive rules will be much more limited in scope and comprehensiveness, defining roughly only the society's institutions and institutional practices. It is therefore possible for an individual to be living in a society and to fall through the gaps, as it were, in the constitutive description—but not in the way that a small boy officially playing in a game of soccer can fall through the gap when all he is doing is wandering about the field of play on his own, trying to keep out of the way of the ball and of the scuffles for it; he has his social equivalent in figures like the tramp, the recluse, and the solitary wino. All of us in our daily lives fall through gaps in the constitutive rules in the different sense that our activities are not determined by, nor describable only in terms of, the rules; all the time we are subject to the regulatory rules of our law, but that is a different matter. Most of what we do does not require our legal institutions for its description: logically it is independent of them and can go on without them; and practically, if only we were nicer people than we are, it could go on without many of our regulatory rules of law as well. If our legal system were suddenly to vanish, then some of our activities and practices would become logically impossible; many more would become much more difficult, but still in principle possible. On the one hand we could not marry, although we could form one-man-one-woman unions, and enduring unions, if we wanted to; we could not vote, we could not litigate, we could not have disputes adjudicated, we could not incur or create obligations as we now can. On the other hand, we could go about our daily lives, on a more primitive level, and probably with far less security, than now, but we could do it; we could have possessions, we could accumulate wealth, we could drive our cars from here to there. And, if the difficulties and risks involved in trying to do those things mounted, as it is to be feared they would, and mounted to the level of impossibility, the impossibility would be causal, not logical. It would be, for an American, like trying to play football with no protective equipment, no officiating referees, judges, etc.; it would not be like trying to play football with no rules about first downs, touchdowns or conversions. The first way, the character of football would change, and change for the worse; the second way, whatever went on would not be football at all.

Because some kind of life in society logically could, and actually might, for a time just limp along in the absence of law, it becomes much more difficult to claim that a person's living in that society, when he is free to leave it but does not, implies his agreement to abide by its laws. The case for claiming that it does is much weaker than it is in the instance of a person participating in a game. And this is reinforced by consideration of the other relevant characteristic of game-playing, that it is a 'contracting in' activity. Nobody finds himself participating in a game, without having in the first place got into it; and in most cases he got into it voluntarily. It is true that in some schools some games are compulsory, where a child is not allowed, without a medical exemption, to escape getting into a game, whenever it is his turn. But being compelled is not the same thing as being in a situation where a question of choice literally does not arise. A military conscript is compelled to report for service, but he is not pressganged; there are other choices which he could take alternative to serving, but they are not choices which he could reasonably be asked to take, or blamed for not taking. That is what compulsion is: being left with only one choice which one could reasonably be asked to take, given the circumstances in which a choice has to be taken. So, even the victim of a system of compulsory games has, when he participates, however unwillingly, in a game, got into it: his activities changed, at a definite time, from not playing in a game to playing in it; his playing had a beginning, preceded by earlier activities. The point being made is that the getting-in or contracting-in aspect of playing in a game is distinct from its being voluntary. And, as most participation in most games is voluntary, most participation possesses both characteristics. Now, it does seem plausible to claim that, if a man gets into an activity which he does not have to, i.e. if he changes from what he is doing to doing something else, and if that something is an activity which he knows to be rule-determined, then that implies, unless he has made a disclaimer, that he has agreed to obey the rules. The claim is at least considerably weakened in the case of the person compelled to play, to the extent that it is accepted that the description of the game as an activity 'which he doesn't have to get into' fails to fit his case; but the claim is strong in the more common case of voluntary participation in the game.

Now, how does the analogy from games fit life in a political society? For some people in some states it fits closely, viz. those who enter as free immigrants, free in the sense that they were not pressured by persecution, destitution or despair to leave their own countries and try their luck elsewhere—if they could find somewhere else to take them in. People who are so pressured are like the victims of compulsory games in that they take their choice to be less unhappy than the alternatives from which they are by it escaping; they are likely to be unlike them in that they will have some hope that the choice which they have been compelled to take will turn out to be one which they will be glad that they were compelled to take. The free immigrant, on the other hand, is like the ordinary games player: he does get into it, and he does get in of his own accord. And, if there is a later step which he is able to take, becoming a citizen of his new country, the same thing will apply over again. In-deed, in a country such as the U.S.A. it is likely to apply to the nonfree immigrant also: when he meets the conditions he becomes eligible for citizenship, but, save for certain profes-sional occupations, he is not subjected to anything approaching compulsion to become a U.S. citizen; if he chooses to do so, he too is, in that respect, acting like a person voluntarily entering a game. And, if there are any people whose conduct can with any plausibility be held to imply agreement to obey the laws of their new country, it will be the new immigrants; not the newly naturalised citizens, because part of their naturalisation process will consist of an explicit undertaking to obey.

So, only one class meets the double condition of voluntarily contracting in, similar to that of the games player, namely the class of free immigrants. But, for any state, they will be a small minority of the total population, the rest of whom did not contract in, let alone voluntarily; like it or not, they were born there, and found themselves in, with nobody having asked first if they wanted to be in. Or they may have been absorbed by conquest or by territorial occupation, e.g. Palestinian Arabs who found Palestine turning into Israel. The former was Socrates' position in Athens, and consequently his merely being there and living in the city could not by itself imply an agree-ment to obey the law. For that reason, Plato introduces the negative choice of not contracting out, and has the laws claim that not contracting out implies agreement, the idea being that voluntarily not contracting out has the same effect as volun-tarily contracting in; the one man does not have to continue his participation, as the other does not have to begin his parti-cipation, so that both are in the same position—both are participating, one because he does not stop, the other because he does begin, and the conduct of both alike implies agreement to obey. With the idea of not contracting out Plato introduces a simple and ingenious device to assimilate the position of the native member of a political society to that of the man who becomes a member by voluntarily joining it. It is not just an 'as if' choice, which is sometimes used in an attempt to bring the obligations of a citizen to political allegiance and obedience under the canopy of the social contract; and it would be weaker if it were. It would be weaker, because 'as if', while it may serve for clarification, cannot provide justification, which is what is wanted here. To say that things are as if *p were* true is to concede that *p* is not true, for things cannot be as if *p were* true if *p* is in fact true. So, if it is claimed that at least for some subjects in some states it is as if they had agreed to obey the laws, that, so far from implying that they did agree, implies that they did not. And, if the point of 'as if' is to suggest that the obligation which they have to obey is like, even very like, the obligation which they would have had if they had agreed, we can reasonably ask why or how. This question will be discussed below, but for the present we can ask the following pair of questions. On what can an obligation be based which will be like an agreement, but is not an agreement? Alternatively, what can be like *being based on* an agreement, but is not *being based on* an agreement? The 'as if' alternatives would in Socrates' case be: (1) his freely staying in the city implied, not an agreement, but something like enough to an agreement for it to be true that it was as if he had agreed; (2) his freely staying in the city did not imply, but did something like enough to implying for it to be true that it was as if it implied an agreement; and logically there could be a third possibility, (3) combining the 'as if' of (1) with that of (2). (1), and hence (3), will not do, because it is repeatedly stressed in the argument that Socrates did agree; and (2), and hence again (3), will not do, because if it was not true that Socrates' staying did imply an agreement, then the question whether there was an agreement would still be open—but, according to the argument it was not open. Consequently, to get from 'Socrates did freely stay' to 'Socrates did agree to obey', the relation between the propositions has, if the argument is to succeed, to be such that from the first the second can be inferred—unless the argument depends on the stronger claim, yet to be considered, that by staying Socrates tacitly agreed, i.e. tacitly expressed his agreement to obey.

The question then has to be asked whether, when a person who is a native born citizen of a state and who is free, in the way in which Socrates was, to contract out but does not, his remaining where he is does imply an agreement to obey the laws of his state. It is surely clear that the mere freely remaining in a jurisdiction does not imply such an agreement, and that the suggestion that it does cannot be supported by argument by analogy from freely joining the jurisdiction. If we take for illustration people living in a modern western society, we can see that the vast majority of them have no public life at all. They have their working life, in which they pursue for so many hours a day whatever occupation they do, and from which they gain the income to support their leisure life, which is whatever they in their circumstances can make it. They may be ready with policy opinions about current economic, political or social issues, but they do nothing about them beyond voting— and many of them do not do that. They pay whatever taxes they cannot avoid, and for the rest they want to be left alone. Their lives and daily conduct are subject to the constraints and the deterrences of their legal system, but they cannot be said to engage in any activity under it remotely similar to the activity which a man begins to engage in when he starts to play a game, such as a game of tennis or of bridge. There has for them never been a point at which they did what could be counted as a minimal agreeing, i.e. embarking on an activity understanding that others expect that the activity will be pursued by each according to the rules, and that nobody has done anything beforehand to disabuse any other of his under- standing. Few of those who are free to go think of themselves, or would think of themselves, as having made, or as continuously renewing, a choice to stay where they are; they simply con- tinue, as best they can, with a way of life with which they are familiar, or they try to reshape it in whatever way seems to them best. The idea that they could go they do not seriously, if at all, entertain; the idea that they have agreed to something, such as to obey the law, or that they have done something which im- plies their agreement they would strenuously deny. They could concur that they ought to obey, and that there are good reasons that they should, even perhaps that the reasons include the sharing of burdens as fair price for sharing of advantages, but that there had ever been anything in their lives which consti- tuted agreement to obey, and which could be inferred from their continuing to stay in their familiar environment, they would surely find a very strange suggestion. It surely is very strange to suggest that a man's continuing with a way of life which he has always lived, which is the only one he has ever known, and to which he feels that he belongs, implies that he has done something in any way similar to what another man does when he voluntarily joins the society in which that way of life is led. The sheer passivity of so many people's relationship and attitude to the laws to which they are subject makes it most implausible to claim that anything about their staying where they are implies that they have agreed to obey.

If we consider interpreting their continuing to stay where they are, even if they are free to go, as implying a continuous process of agreement to obey, will the theory fare better? There is the question of the condition of freedom itself, which is one of varying complexities and dimensions, but that will be left alone for the present. That apart, what does the idea of a continuing process of agreement come to? It would have to be a continuing process of unexpressed agreement for, otherwise, the principle of implied agreement would, in this case, collapse into the principle of tacit (at least) agreement. And the idea of a man continuously agreeing, but never expressing his agreement, and of his staying as implying his continuously agreeing, is surely a very odd one. One might attempt to make it more palatable to reason by interpreting it in a hypothetical way— viz. that, if certain conduct is what one would have agreed to if given the choice under free conditions of opportunity and power, then one is bound to that conduct even although there was no actual agreement. The general principle there is that, if x is what you would have agreed to, had you been in the position of having to decide whether to agree or not, then x is what you ought to do, even though, as it happens, you did not agree to do it; as long as it is what you would have agreed to do, had you had the chance to agree, it does not cease to be what you should do, just because you did not have the chance to agree, e.g. because you happened not to be there at the time. How can it be reasonable to refuse to do x, if you admit that x is what you would have agreed to do, had you been there at the time? This line of argument does seem to have some air of plausibility about it; and it might appear also to be a main line of argument pursued by John Rawls in his influential book *A Theory of Justice*.[1] He presents his theory as being a social con-

[1] John Rawls, *A Theory of Justice* (Cambridge, Mass.: Belknap Press, 1971).

tract theory, and confronts us with a group of people subjected
to certain conditions which will make their deliberations and
decisions purely rational, and faced with the question of deciding what principles they would want to have as the basic principles for a society in which they were going to live, what
principles they could agree with each other to be bound by.
'The contract doctrine is purely hypothetical; if a conception
of justice would be agreed to in the original position, its principles are the right ones to apply. It is no objection that such an
understanding has never been nor ever will be entered into.'[1]
'The merit of the contract terminology is that it conceives the
idea that principles of justice may be conceived as principles
that would be chosen by rational persons, and that in this way
conceptions of justice may be explained and justified.'[2] And,
speaking of 'the principles of natural duty and obligation that
apply to individuals', he writes 'we must now consider why
these principles would be chosen in the original position. They
are an essential part of a conception of right: they define our
institutional ties and how we become bound to one another.'[3]
Those three passages are typical of many others that could be
chosen from the book. Each of the first two discloses an ambiguity in the claim that x is what we ought to do, or a principle
which we ought to adopt, because it is what we would have
agreed to do or to adopt, had we had the chance to agree. But
the third passage indicates which of the two interpretations of
Rawls's argument is correct, and that it is *not* the line of argument suggested earlier as the line which he might appear to be
following; and the error contained in that line of argument is
such that the argument would not do as one about agreement
for the laws to use against Socrates. The claim that one ought
to do x, because x is what one would have agreed to, had one
had the chance of doing it, either is invalid or has nothing
essentially to do with agreement, even hypothetical agreement.
It is invalid if it supposes that a hypothetical agreement is an
agreement, or has the force of one. If one agrees to do a certain
thing, then there is one reason that one ought to do it, and there
may be two. There will be at least the one reason, viz. that one

[1] Ibid., p. 167.
[2] Ibid., p. 16.
[3] Ibid., p. 333.

did agree to do it, one did authorise the other party to expect performance. But that reason will operate only in the case where one actually did agree. This can easily be seen by taking a case where the fact of having agreed is the only reason why one ought to do the thing in question. Suppose a group of friends, say members of a tennis club, decide to run a winner-take-all sweepstake on the outcome of a certain horse race; they agree that each will contribute $1 to the pool and draw a ticket which will either be a blank or bear the name of one of the horses in the race, and that the one who turns out to have drawn the winning horse scoops the pool. They do this, and John Smith wins. Subsequently, another member of the club, who had been absent at the time when the sweepstake was organised and executed, and so had been unable to participate, is asked whether he would have participated, had he been present. When he replies that he would, he would be astonished, and rightly astonished, to be told that, as he would have agreed to contribute $1 to the winner's prize, he ought to give John Smith $1 now. (More details are needed to make the story watertight, but it is unnecessary to give them here for the general purpose of the illustration.) If *the* reason that I ought to do a certain thing is that I agreed to, then it cannot be operative in the case where I did not agree to; and it makes no difference that I would have agreed, had I been asked. I may be lucky or unlucky, as the case may be, not to have been asked. So, if the laws were saying to Socrates that *the* reason that a citizen of Athens should obey the laws was that he had agreed to, and that, in the cases where he had not agreed (because an occasion for agreeing had not arisen), he still should obey, if it was true that he would have agreed had the occasion arisen, then their line of argument would be invalid. The counterfactual 'I would have agreed, if . . .' does not have the binding force which 'I do agree' does: agreeing is a performance which does authorise expectation and hence binds, but the counterfactual that one would have agreed if . . . is not a performance at all, and there is nothing there to authorise expectation or to bind.

What makes one uneasy about admitting the invalidity of 'You ought to do it, because you would have agreed to do it, had you had the chance' is that there are plenty of cases where we do agree to do something, and where we *correctly* think of somebody else who did not agree to do it (because he did not have the chance of agreeing) that he ought to do it, because it is something which he would have agreed to do, if he had had the chance of agreeing; and to admit the latter seems to be inconsistent with insisting on the invalidity of the former. But it is not, and its appearance of being so derives from the ambiguity previously referred to. So far we have considered only the case of agreement, where there is one reason only for doing what one has agreed to do, viz. that one has agreed to do it. But in many cases there are two reasons, that one plus whatever reason there is *for* agreeing to do it. (There can be more than two reasons, but they are all that fall to be considered here.) What is a good reason that some thing should be done can also be a good reason for agreeing to do it. If there is a good reason for members of an office staff to do what they can to help another fellow member suddenly faced with a grave personal problem, emergency or expense, it can be a good reason for their agreeing to help. And, if they do agree to help, then there are two reasons that they ought to help: (1) that they agreed to, and (2) the reason for their agreeing to. Now, although (1) cannot operate if they did not agree, (2) can: it is independent of actual agreement, for it is the reason for agreeing (if they actually do), and it is the reason for doing the thing, in this case helping the fellow worker, whether or not one agreed to help. This reason that one ought to help does apply to the person who had not agreed to help (because, e.g., he was not there at the time when the rest of the office staff agreed), and it is not tied to agreement; it is a reason for one member of the office giving help to another member who needs it, even if the former had not been a party to the agreement to help. Reminding somebody that helping is something he would have agreed to, had he been in a position to do so, can be a pointed way of reminding him that there is a good reason for helping, and that it is what would have been a good reason for agreeing to help, had he been in a position to agree. That is the line of argument pursued by Rawls, when he says that certain principles of justice are the right ones to apply if they are the ones which belong to a conception of justice that would be agreed to in the original position, and that the merit of the contract terminology is that it presents principles of justice as principles that would be chosen by rational process. It may be objected that it is hardly a merit of contract *terminology* (his word), because the terminology suggests that the idea of a contract or agreement, whether actual or hypothetical, is central to the theory, when in fact it is not; what is central is the idea of something as *that which* would have been chosen or agreed to (if anything had been), and why it would have. The 'why' of the matter is the reason for choosing or agreeing to *that*, not the reason for *choosing or agreeing to* that.

In 52c–d the laws make an interesting switch in their line of argument against Socrates. In 51d–52b the line had been the one so far discussed: (a) that any citizen of Athens who remains in the city when, if he prefers, he is free to go, has agreed to do what the laws order him to do; and (b) that Socrates himself has, for the reasons stated, stood out among other Athenians as a man who has agreed in that way. It is the fact of staying that makes it correct to say that he has agreed. And it is the fact of staying in what might be called the strong sense— not just staying where he is when it is possible and permissible to go, but actually refusing the opportunity of going. The Greek word παραμένειν is a stronger word than the unprefixed μένειν, and commonly has the meaning of standing fast, standing one's ground: in this case Socrates had let go by every opportunity he had of leaving, and what in consequence he had agreed to do was to obey the laws. Παραμένειν is contrasted with ἀποδιδράσκειν, 'to run away' (e.g., *Meno* 97d), and is used of a faithful slave who remains with his master, rather than run away; and that may be the point of the remark to Socrates that, if he tries to escape, he will be doing the same thing as the lowest kind of slave (52d, cf. 50a).

The new move comes in 52c, where Socrates is told something else, that what he had agreed to do was πολιτεύεσθαι, which is something more than just doing whatever he was ordered by the laws to do. The word *can* mean as little as just living in the city, but its much more usual sense is that of participating in the life of the city, playing one's part as a citizen. The picture is no longer that of the subject dutifully complying with the law, but instead that of the individual making his contribution to the life of the state. And the case for saying that somebody in that position has an obligation, based on agreement, to obey the law is much stronger. Socrates is now represented as a man who not merely had throughout a long lifetime unbrokenly resided in the city but also had participated in a citizen's way of life, and as having agreed to continue that participation, the ground for saying that he had agreed being that he had let go by all the opportunities he had of leaving. The analogy with playing a game comes closer again, for playing his part as a citizen is something which a man does begin to do, not at a time perhaps, but over a period of time; and, although not many games provide for giving up and dropping out in the course of play, unless forced to by injury, some do, and across a wide range, e.g., from long-distance running to poker. And it is arguable that people who do engage in activities which are institutionalised can be taken, as long as they continue to engage in them (if they are genuinely free to resign), as having agreed to abide by the rules of the activity, and indeed by the rulings of the authority, as long as it itself shows enough respect for the rules. If a body, e.g., the teaching staff of a university, has, within whatever limits, some autonomy, then (to continue with the example) members of the staff may be seen as having a contractual or consensual obligation to pursue and to promote the academic activities of the university, including abiding by the body's rules and indeed the dean's rulings—as long at least as those are seen as being in harmony with the body's purposes and functions. Neither rules nor ruler have a blank cheque: what the members of the body have agreed to do in agreeing to obey the ruler is not, as pointed out earlier, to do whatever the ruler tells them to do, no matter what, but is to do what he tells them to do, where that is consonant with the aims, procedures and general point of the activity or activities in which they are participating. If 'rocking the boat' had not become an easy catch phrase for a fearful establishment to use against those within its domain who show a distressing eagerness for change, it would do as a characterisation of what participants in an ongoing activity, such as playing their part in their university's or their state's way of life, may be taken as having agreed not to do. There is a considerable difference between, on the one hand, being within the realm of a jurisdiction and so being subject to its laws, like it or not, as long as one stays there, and, on the other hand, participating, in however small a way, in the institutionalised life of the society. Given that that requires conformity with the rules of law, then anybody who participates and continues to participate, freely, when there is an alternative which he could adopt but does not, and who, as he knows, is known by others to be freely participating must be taken to have agreed to participate—not, it should be repeated, to participate no matter what, but to participate as long as either he does not contract out or rules, ruler and indeed the other participants in general conform to the principles holding at the time of, or over the period of, his agreement. It is not difficult to believe that Socrates, as presented in the *Crito*, met those conditions, and was therefore properly held by the laws to have agreed to obey them.

What is not clear is whether Plato presented Socrates' agreement as being one of implied or of tacit agreement. The likely truth is that he never thought of the difference between them, and consequently that the question of presenting Socrates as belonging with the one rather than the other never entered his head. Nor are we any better off in this case if we ask what do his words mean rather than what did he mean by them. All that we can get out of them is that there was an agreement, and that it was not an explicit verbal one. He used the aorist tense, 'you did agree', enough to suggest that there was a time at which Socrates supposedly agreed—which in turn suggests a performance that counts as agreeing; but he also as often used the perfect tense, 'you have agreed'—which suggests that an agreement was implied by his continued life in Athens. But neither does more than suggest what it does, and each cancels the other out. So, if we have to ask which of the two did Plato mean rather than the other, we do best to answer 'Neither'. And for his purpose he did not need to answer the question. Either way, if the laws' assertion was correct, Socrates had agreed to obey, and either, therefore, generated his duty to obey, which was all that they were concerned to establish. But still, for the sake of completeness, and because the question has an interest on its own, we should consider whether *we* should take Socrates, on the story as given in the *Crito*, to be an example of the one rather than the other, basing an answer, not

on what is or is not said in 51–2 about agreement, but on what
is or is not said about the conduct which implies or constitutes
it. What is the difference between implied agreement and tacit
agreement? And can we say on which side of it Socrates, as
described by Plato, falls? We might be able to answer that,
although unable to say on which side of it Plato described
Socrates as falling.

Nothing can be made out of the point, brought in twice, that
the agreeing was done by action rather than by words. For,
although that does eliminate explicit verbal agreement,
uttered in speech or in writing, it does not discriminate between
implied and tacit agreement. It has so far been argued that
staying, as Socrates did, in a political society when genuinely
free to go, where staying consists, not just of remaining there,
but also of staying there *as* a citizen, playing some part in the
state-citizen relationship, does at least imply agreement to
abide by the society's laws. So, in Socrates' case we do have at
least implied agreement: his continuing to live in Athens, and
to live the life he did, did show that he had agreed to obey the
laws, that being part of what it was to live the life of a citizen.
But that his staying showed his agreement is one thing. That by
staying he showed his agreement would be another; and, unless
we can find *at least* that, we cannot justifiably assert that he
tacitly agreed, i.e. that by some nonverbal conduct he expressed his agreement. There is absolutely nothing in the text
to direct us to the conclusion that he did tacitly express his
agreement. The only passage about showing (52b1–2) concerns
not his agreement to obey the law, but his satisfaction with the
city and its laws; and it is a passage which unequivocally talks
of Socrates' conduct showing his satisfaction ($\mu\epsilon\gamma\acute{a}\lambda a$ $\dot{\eta}\mu\hat{\iota}\nu$
$\tau\epsilon\kappa\mu\acute{\eta}\rho\iota\acute{a}$ $\dot{\epsilon}\sigma\tau\iota\nu$), not at all of his showing his satisfaction.
Furthermore, a man might show that he agreed without there-
by expressing his agreement; and therefore, even if we could
say that a man in Socrates' circumstances, who behaved as
Socrates did, showed that he agreed to obey the laws, we could
not necessarily on that account say that he expressed his agreement to obey. This can be illustrated by an example from
wanting, where the distinctions come out very clearly. Suppose
there is a question whether A wants to buy a new car. Now,
there could be evidence that he does: he has been observed

staring in showroom windows, reading motoring magazines, lingering over newspaper advertisements, asking questions about particular kinds of car, etc.—none of those being things which he ordinarily does at all. And, if the evidence was good enough in quantity and quality, we could infer something at least about his hankering after a new car; his behaviour suggests (and in a favourable case shows or implies) that he is hankering after a new car. Suppose now that there is more to the story: not only is there evidence that he wants the car but he himself puts the evidence in our way, does what he can to make sure that we do not miss it. His behaviour now consists both of behaving as in the first story and of behaving in a way which calls attention to that behaviour. Now we can say that he shows us by his behaviour that he wants the new car, for he *intends* us to notice his behaviour which is evidence that he wants it, and to see it *as* evidence that he wants it. We might even say that he as good as told us that he wanted it, but it would in fact be some way short of telling, because he has not yet done anything that would count as communicating. He intends us to notice the relevant parts of his behaviour, he intends to make sure that we notice them, and he intends us to see them as evidence that he wants the car. But his enterprise, to be successful, does not require any of the conventions required for communication, and particularly does not require that we *recognise* that he does intend us to do what he intends us to do. For his intention to succeed we do not have to suppose that he is trying to get any message across to us at all. The difference between the first and the second case is that in the first case we inferred from his behaviour that he wanted the new car, while in the second case he saw to it that we inferred from his behaviour that he wanted the new car, In the first case his behaviour showed that he wanted it, in the second case he showed by his behaviour that he wanted it; but not even in the second case can he be said to have expressed to us his desire for a new car. The third case (given in detail below), which is a case of communicating by expressing his desire, is also commonly called his showing us that he has the desire, but it is showing in a different way from the second case, differing from it in the respect in which the second resembles the first. Those two resemble each other, in that in each case we can tell from

H

the man's behaviour that he wants the car, while in neither is there any question of his telling us that he wants it. In what would be the fourth case, that in which he in so many words informed us that he wanted the car, he tells us that he wants it, but it would be inappropriate, except in special circumstances, to say that we can tell from what he says that he wants the car. If what he says is that he wants the car, then we do not, in the ordinary case, have to tell from that that he wants it—it is not an occasion for telling in that sense, or inferring at all. Our third case is that in which, without actually telling us in so many words that he wants the car, he does try to communicate to us his desire, he does, by whatever behaviour will do it, express his desire[1] for the car. Here again, unless there is some question about his sincerity, or his tendency to self-deception, if he, by whatever behaviour, expresses his desire for the car, it is inappropriate to say that we tell or infer from that that he wants the car. If he really is trying to express his desire for the car, it would be at least extremely rude to ask him whether we can tell or infer from that that he wants the car. Expressing a desire for the car is as much a way of communicating to us that he wants the car as is his explicitly telling us that he wants it. Now, what formally does expressing a desire require? It requires, at least, trying to get the other person to believe that one has the desire by his recognising one's intention to get him to believe that, i.e. it involves trying to get across or convey to him one's intention that he believe that; and consequently it requires the use of understood or understandable conventions for communicating the expression of the desire. Expressing something *to* somebody is as convention-dependent as is any other way of communicating, the most common, convenient and flexible way being by the use of speech-utterances and written (printed, etc.) utterances. In the absence of conventions for expressing desires, there would be no way of successfully expressing a desire. In the absence of a convention one could *try* to express a desire to another, but one could succeed only by inducing the other to formulate the hypothesis (or by him formulating it for himself) that what one was trying to do was to set up a pattern of behaviour *as* a convention for ex-

---

[1] See above, p. 80, n. 1.

pressing the desire, and then by confirming the hypothesis, if he formulates the correct one, via another communication-convention. If the other party has no suspicion, and cannot be induced to have one, that some communication is being attempted, the enterprise of communicating cannot even begin. Fortunately, with a little intelligence and a little imagination, people are very quick to learn. One can see somebody make quite a complicated shopping request in a foreign country, where shopper and assistant have not a word of any language in common, and the communication can, after very little trial and error, be successfully conveyed by rapidly tried out and picked up conventions. The whole business can be triumphantly concluded with short cuts and with a speed which only a linguist would believe to be impossible.

Now, that has everything to do with expressing being a way of communicating, nothing to do with what was, in the illustration, being expressed being a desire. Although communication can be quickly established, because conventions can, if they do not already exist, be quickly set up and recognised, they must either be set up or already exist, and they must be recognised. So, Socrates, by his staying and participating as a citizen, cannot have been tacitly expressing his agreement to participate, including obedience to the laws, unless he was using recognised or recognisable conventions for doing that. Whether there were appropriate communication conventions in the Athens of his day, and he used them, or whether he successfully tried out conventions of his own we cannot tell. All that we can say is that, unless one or other was the case, he could not have tacitly agreed to obey the law. He may, as the laws in the *Crito* say he did, by his actions have agreed to obey, but the agreement would be one implied by his conduct, not one tacitly expressed by it. If Socrates had been by staying tacitly agreeing to obey, it is highly unlikely that he would have been introducing a convention for communicating his expression of agreement, since so many thousands of citizens before him had stayed in sufficiently similar circumstances. There would almost certainly be an established convention by which staying was understood as expressing agreement to obey; and the laws, in addressing Socrates, might have been expected to remind him of that. Therefore, on the admittedly meagre supply of clues provided on pages 51–2, it seems reasonable to conclude that a man in a situation as Socrates' was described to be, and who had behaved as Socrates was described as having behaved, should be taken to have behaved in a way which implied, but did not express, agreement to obey the law. In the absence of clear indications either of existing conventions for communicating agreement or of the agent trying to set up and use one himself, we do not have enough to attribute tacit agreement to a man in that situation.

Something remains to be said about freedom. The laws do not in this passage remind Socrates that, as he has agreed to obey, the agreement is binding. They do not remind him of that, because they do not need to; it was he himself who had earlier insisted that one must stick to one's agreements, provided that they are just. If the laws are technically begging the question, in that they have not argued for the proposition that what he has agreed to do in agreeing to obey the laws is just, it might be said that, by the persuade-or-obey doctrine, and by the claim that the laws are reasonable rather than despotic in their requirements, they are paying sufficient attention to it and therefore need not actually mention it. But what about the requirement of freedom? An agreement does not have to be free to be an agreement, but it does have to be free to be a valid agreement, one by which the party imposes on himself the obligation to fulfil the agreement. Questions begin to arise when we ask what is to count as being or not being free, and about the spectrum of freedom—how free is free? The restrictions on Socrates' freedom are represented as being nil; and, whether or not we could agree with that, we could agree that anybody would be fortunate who had as few. There were no legal restrictions: as a citizen he was allowed by law to stay or to emigrate, just as he pleased. There were no financial restrictions: he was allowed to take with him whatever he possessed. He was not forced into the agreement, he was not tricked into it, and he did not have to make up his mind in a hurry, without sufficient time for reflection. All those factors count heavily in favour of the thesis that Socrates was free in agreeing to obey the law; if he was not free, would anybody ever be? And yet to leave those factors as just presented would be oversimple: although under each heading there may have been no restrictions on Socrates' freedom, yet, without alteration in the headings, there could be restrictions the effect of which (and sometimes, in the case of legal freedom, the design of which) would be to diminish to a lesser or greater degree the subject's freedom. A state may not impose a legal ban on emigration, while at the same time its regulations under the emigration law may make it extremely difficult, and even for some impossible, to go. As a simple illustration, a birth certificate may be required. For many people that presents no problem, for they either have a copy or know how to go about getting one. But some, who do not have a copy, may have no idea how to go about getting one and may have enormous physical obstacles in the way of finding out, e.g. they live miles from anywhere, have never heard of Citizens' Advice Bureaus or the like (and there may be no such things in their state or town), and know nobody whose advice they can seek; others again could find procuring a birth certificate quite impossible, because they were born abroad and requests to the authorities in their native state (if it still exists) go unanswered. The assertion that the law allows anyone who wishes to leave may be true, at the same time as the assertion that the law does not prevent anyone who wishes to from leaving is false. And that, so far, is only a matter of the conditions laid down by law. They can be, and often are, compounded in the application of law by bureaucratic incompetence, petti-fogginess, or straightforward obstructionism; there are many ways of failing to get an exit permit besides the official refusal of one. It is interesting to note that, if Athenian law is accurately represented by the account given in the *Crito*, a citizen such as Socrates would have had no trouble with the law in moving away from the city, if he had wished, for it is asserted that the law neither *forbids* nor does anything to *obstruct* emigration (51d). The variety of ways in which the law can obstruct, while correctly insisting that it does not forbid, has been improved since his time. Another restriction, diminishing the freedom to go (and consequently the freedom of the agreement), which apparently Socrates would not have had to face, but which confronts almost all would-be emigrants today, is that imposed, not by the law of the country to be left, but by that of the country to be entered. In 52b it is suggested that, if Socrates were to avoid execution by fleeing from Athens to a neighbouring state governed by good laws, such as Thebes or Megara, he would there be regarded as an enemy of the state, and under suspicion as a destroyer of the laws—but nothing is said about his being expelled or being refused entry; clearly then he would have been received there without difficulty, had his departure from Athens been legal. But the modern immigrant is unlikely to be so lucky; he may have to find his way, if he can, through a minefield of immigration quotas, work permits, health examinations, police checks, even in a country as openarmed as the U.S.A.; elsewhere the requirements, especially those concerned with political activity, can be anything but welcoming. Being legally free to leave one's own country is only half, and often the easier half, of being free to emigrate; being free to get in somewhere else is the other half. Whatever legal restriction is placed on either is a diminution of one's legal freedom to move. And, as one has to be legally free to move, if staying is to be fully legally free, and with it the agreement to obey the law which staying (in the full, participatory sense, in which Socrates stayed) may be said to imply, the conduct of few people anywhere today can be seen as implying a fully free agreement.

But let us suppose the case of a man for whom there are no legal restrictions whatever either on his leaving his country or on his entering and taking up residence in the country of his choice. Is he then free to go? If all that is to be meant by the assertion that he is free is that he is *allowed* to go, then, of course he is free. And that is one sense in which 'free' is used. But there can be many circumstances in which it is a mockery of freedom to tell a man that he is free to do a certain thing, if he wants, where the only freedom he has is freedom from legal prohibition or obstruction. The other obstacles to freedom can be summarily grouped together under the heading of costs, of which some, but not all, can be literally costed in financial terms—the cost of the journey from old to new domicile, the removal costs, the resettlement costs, etc., plus whatever has to be given up or forgone in order to provide the money to meet those costs. The extreme, but far from imaginary, case is that of the man who simply has not got, and could not raise, the money needed to move himself, let alone his family, from where he is to where he would, if he could, choose to be. It is surely grotesquely false to tell a man just released from gaol, without a job and without funds, that, if he does not like the way things are managed here, he is free to go somewhere else—there is nothing to stop him; and consequently that his staying is to be interpreted as implying his agreement to obey laws such as that for the infraction of which he has just completed his sentence. It is not true that there is nothing to stop him; there is no policeman barring the way, but the way is not cleared simply by the removal of the policeman. And ranging down from that extreme case are all those who are not totally unable to raise the money, but can do it only by imposing hardships of varying degrees of severity on themselves, and especially on others, such as their family. Freedom is not an either-or matter, but one of degrees: some people, due to their financial circumstances and commitments, are less free than others. When a man's financial commitments include the support of others, on whom he would impose great hardship if he withdrew the support, as he might be forced to if he left the country, he is not as free to go as the man whose going would impose hardship only on himself. The schoolteacher struggling to keep his head just above the rising waters of inflation, with the mortgage payments to keep up and a wife and two children to feed and clothe, is less free to go than the property speculator with the comfortable cushion of a Swiss bank account or funds in the Bahamas. Although the teacher, we shall suppose, could just make it, we could understand his saying that fifteen years ago he might have done it, but now it is too late; that is a way of saying that he does not have the freedom which he once had.

Included among the costs of freedom are those that cannot be costed—the breaks in family ties, and in cultural ties, and the wrench of leaving home for a strange place and an alien way of life—in general all that has to be given up, and what has to be accepted in replacement of it. For very many people transplanting can be a serious operation, and for many too serious to be faced. Can we then really say of the man held back by all those ties to a place and a way of life to which he feels that he belongs that he is free to go—or as free as the man with no such ties? Or should we say that they have nothing to do with his freedom, that, if there are no legal obstacles, and if the means of going are available, then he is free—and that all those other factors go, not to the question whether he is free, but to the question whether he ought to *feel* free, or even whether he *can* feel free, to go? The latter does seem an oversimple view of freedom. For, how do those factors differ relevantly from the pressures which reach their extreme in duress or coercion, and would then negate freedom? Being coerced or compelled to do *x* is not a matter of doing *x* in circumstances in which there is literally no alternative action. There always is an alternative, but it is one which the agent could not possibly or reasonably be expected to choose. And for that reason it is an error to represent moral action, action for a moral reason, as always being free action; moral reasons can be as compelling as those of fear or prudence. Attempts at coercion or duress do not work unless they get to the man: to be compelled he must feel compelled. Indeed, being compelled is feeling compelled in circumstances in which it is reasonable or proper to feel compelled; and the pressures which are somewhat less than those amounting to absolute compulsion are less in degree, not different in character—and so on down the line. And somewhat correspondingly with freedom. At one level, to be free to go is to be in a position and actually to feel free in it: if the man does not feel free, he is not freed from the pressures which tell on him; in that sense being free requires feeling free. What this shows is that a question of freedom is a question about assessment of fact, not just a question of fact. When we assert that the man is free to go, or that there is nothing to stop him, we are asserting that there is no reason, or not good enough reason, for him to feel that there is anything stopping him; and to tell him that he is free, when he insists that he is not (or *vice versa*) is to encourage him, if we can, to feel differently and more appropriately than he does.

What the argument comes to is that, although Socrates probably was, as the laws claimed he was, free to leave Athens, if he wished, his freedom was determined not solely by the factors mentioned in the text of the *Crito*; and that, if all of them are taken into account, he was especially favoured—he was free to an extent to which very few of mankind now are. If people's staying where they are is less than fully free, then an agreement to obey the law implied by their staying is less than

fully free, and their obligation to obedience deriving from the
agreement is that much the less. This is not to say (nor to deny)
that in the conditions of modern states subjects have a diminished
obligation to obey the laws of their system. But it is to say that
the model of the social contract is an unsatisfactory one for
explaining or clarifying obligation to obey the law; we have
either to find the obligation elsewhere or to abandon the claim
that most of us any longer have it.

One final point should be made. Even if the agreement to
stay as a participating citizen, which will include obedience
to law, is valid, as in Socrates' case it was, and hence engenders
an obligation to obey, that does not necessarily end the matter.
Socrates half suggests that it does not (52c1–2), but immediately
drops the idea. But it should not be dropped: where there is an
obligation, it can, without being the less an obligation, be
overriden by another; or it can be overtaken by changes in
circumstance or in knowledge about them, foresight of which
was not available at the time when the obligation was incurred,
making its performance impossible, or the demand for it un-
conscionable. Furthermore, as already argued (pp. 24–5),
although there is a valid agreement, the obligation carried by it
has its limits, so that demands for performance outside the limits
bear no obliging force. If a man has agreed to do what the law
tells him to do (provided that what he has agreed to do in agreeing to do what the law tells him to do is just), he does not thereby
give the law a blank cheque in telling him what to do. The
impotent and fearful government of a country occupied in wartime may by law require mayors and regional officials to hand
over a regular quota of ablebodied men to the occupying
power, to provide slave labour for munitions factories in the
occupying power's homeland, but the officials have no moral
obligation to do it; that is not included within the scope of
what they agreed to when they agreed to apply and to enforce
the law. The effect is the same as that achieved by Socrates'
own principle that one must do whatever he has agreed to do,
provided that it is just. And he could have argued that abiding
by the verdict and sentence of an unjust and politically fixed
trial was not among the things that he had agreed to in agreeing to obey the law. As it was, Socrates accepted a quite
different reason why he ought to accept the court decision,

unjust though it was, viz. that not to do so would be an act of destruction, it would be to strike at the law, in the first place at the particular law involved, that requiring that all court findings be upheld. If that is a good reason that the law should be obeyed, it is so independently of any agreement made to obey the law. If disobedience is destructive, and if the duty to obey derives from an agreement, then disobedience may indeed be destructive of the whole rule of law, including the system of agreement from which, on that view, law derives its binding force. But the thesis that disobedience is destructive of law does not depend on law's deriving its legitimacy from an agreement. Even if there is no such thing as an agreement, it might still be true that disobedience to law is destructive of it. And therefore, although it is not presented as a separate argument in the *Crito*, but as a thread running through the other two arguments, it is a separate argument, and will be discussed in the next chapter.

CHAPTER SIX

Disobedience as Destructive of Law

The claim that to break the law is to destroy the law is a
familiar theme of public rhetoric. It is used against campaigns
of civil disobedience, and it is brought in as a final denunciation
of illegal strikes. But it requires much closer examination than
it receives from those who proclaim it in their speeches, because
it is far too general, if left at that, to be either agreed or dis-
agreed with. When the various forms into which it can be
specified are carefully distinguished from each other, it will be
found that some have to be rejected as downright false or
unworthy of consideration, others are at most vacuously true,
leaving two forms to be taken seriously; and one of those is
misleadingly characterised as a 'destructive of law' form at all.
There is the question too whether it can be determined which,
if any, of them can be found in the *Crito*.

The thesis that Socrates, if he goes through with the plan to
frustrate the court's sentence by making a last minute escape,
will destroy the law, recurs throughout the address which he
imagines the laws of Athens making to him, but it is nowhere
developed into a separate argument on its own. The references
are brief, but they do allow the elimination of some of the
cruder versions of the theme that lawbreaking is destructive of
the law. The theme will be either consequential or noncon-
sequential in character, and the cruder versions will all be of
the consequential kind. The theme will be consequential if it
maintains, in one form or another, that breakdown in the law
will be produced by disobedience to the law. The proposition
being asserted there is a causal one, viz. that an effect of disobedience will be that the law is destroyed; and as a causal
proposition it, again in whatever form it takes, is to be accepted or rejected on the empirical evidence of what actually
does happen in cases where the law is broken. Causal proposi-

tions, especially of a sociological kind, are notoriously difficult
to verify, and, because they are, come very easily to the lips of
public speakers, who can get away with totally unsupported
generalisations without any serious risk of immediate or even
early refutation; the evidence against such a generalisation is
as hard to come by as the evidence for it. Thus, confident
pronouncements on the effects of television programs (e.g., sex,
violence) on their audiences, especially their young audiences,
or on the overall effects of varying styles and methods of education can be made with a security beyond the reach of any
hypothesis about, say, correlation between cigarette smoking
and lung cancer. Their influence on opinion is proportional,
not to the value of the evidence provided, but to the precon-
ceptions and prejudices which they fit. Intellectually, they are
usually worthless, because, where human behaviour and condi-
tioning are involved, the factors are so variable, the possibilities
of controlled experiments approaching anywhere near labora-
tory rigour are so restricted, and the amounts of time (extending
over a generation or more), trouble and money required are so
vast that it is hardly surprising if nothing more respectable than
tentative and appropriately vague conclusions can be expected.
In the area of human conduct, above all areas, causal propositions, especially general causal propositions, call for a more
cautious scepticism than they commonly receive.

The simple claim that a single act of lawbreaking by a single
individual (e.g., Socrates), will have as its immediate effect the
collapse, like the walls of Jericho, either of the particular law
broken or of the system of law to which it belongs, is too silly to
take seriously; and there is not a hint of it in the *Crito*. It is silly,
because there is all the evidence in the world against it. There
are countless such acts in every jurisdiction every day; and if,
to preserve the parallel with Socrates, we reduce the number by
restricting ourselves to just those acts of lawbreaking which are
detected and successfully prosecuted, we still have plenty on
our hands. If the proposition were true, and any such act had
that effect, then there would be no laws nor legal systems cur-
rently in existence; but there are; therefore the proposition is
clearly false. If we try as an alternative the proposition that
such a single act will eventually produce a collapse in the law,
we can see how it might be true—provided that a number of

other conditions were also fulfilled. No subject's act of illegality will by itself bring down the law that is broken, or the system to which it belongs, but it *might* do it, if the example of illegality, especially of successful illegality, were to encourage others to do likewise, and if the practice became sufficiently widespread. But for that to happen many other things are needed. The agent must be in, or be by publicity thrust into, a position of some prominence, if his conduct is going to encourage others to act similarly; otherwise they will not know of his act, or will not pay attention to it. What an American President, a British Prime Minister, or the leader of an internationally known pop group does will receive notice; what an inconspicuous member of the public does will not. But it is not enough that he be prominent: he must also be regarded with some admiration, or respect or affection by those whose conduct his example is going to influence. Thus, on the one hand a popular rock singer's drugtaking may be copied by many of his followers, and on the other hand President Nixon ends in solitary isolation. No doubt, any public illegality by Socrates would have attracted far more attention in Athens (as any public illegality by Bertrand Russell would have done in England) than the same illegality committed by a nobody. But, unless Socrates was much more of a popular hero than the outcome of his trial suggests that he was, and unless also the public climate of the time was fairly favourable to an illegality of that particular kind, his escape would not likely have started a rot in prison security.

A law is inefficacious if people will not adhere to it, and if it either cannot be or is not enforced, so that non-adherence can be pursued with success or impunity. A simple illustration is provided by the contempt with which a capital city's parking regulations are treated by members of accredited foreign missions, whose diplomatic immunity protects them from prosecution. In a positivistic sense the regulations still exist and apply to the diplomatic sector of the population, but, as long as that sector chooses to ignore them, and is allowed to do so with immunity, their applicability to that sector can be said to have been destroyed. A more egregious instance would be the farcical fate of prohibition in the U.S.A., where disregard of the law and connivance at the disregard became so wide-

spread that the only decent fate to accord to the 18th Amendment was to repeal it; this was done by the 21st Amendment
in 1933.

It is noticeable that in the *Crito* the laws make little use of the
thesis that the destruction of a law will follow as a consequence
of sufficiently widespread breaking of it. It is mentioned only
once (50b), in a passage which is marked by its being the one
and only time that destruction of a single law (τούτου τοῦ νόμου)
is mentioned, and by its being the one and only time that
destruction by general disregard (as in the parking and prohibition examples) is mentioned: Socrates is asked whether it is
possible for a city to exist and not to be overturned, in which
court decisions do not prevail, but are invalidated and destroyed by the actions of private individuals. All other passages
are directly pointed at Socrates: is *he* intending to destroy the
laws (50b, cf. 51a)? What charge has *he* against them that he
is trying to destroy them (50d, cf. 52c)? And, if he escapes and
goes to a well-governed city such as Thebes or Megara he will
be regarded with suspicion as a destroyer of the laws (53b).
Secondly, the object of destruction in those and other passages
is not a particular law, but the laws in general (in several passages the laws and the city). So, in the *Crito* there is no consideration (with the one exception already mentioned) of what
will happen if there is sufficiently widespread breaking of one
particular law. And there is no consideration of what will
happen if there is sufficiently widespread breaking of the laws
in general. There is perhaps a hint of it in the question 'For
who could be satisfied with a city that had no laws?' (53a). The
main interest of that question is that it appears to imply that a
city could *exist* without laws. For there is no point in asking
whether anyone would want to live in a city without laws, if
such a city were impossible. And yet the implication seems
inconsistent with the claim already mentioned, that a city
could not exist if its court decisions were not upheld. The
thought there has to be that at least some laws are necessary
to a city's existence, namely those concerned with trial procedure and adjudication. The passages can perhaps be recon-
ciled, if in the earlier one the phrase about the impossibility of
such a city *existing* is understood as being about the impossibility
of its *surviving*, or continuing to exist.

In any case, the charge against Socrates is that, if he goes through with the planned break from prison, he will be destroying, or trying to destroy, the laws. And one further qualification has to be made. In two passages the question put is, not whether he intends to destroy, nor whether he is going to try to destroy, the laws, but whether he intends to do it 'for your part' (τὸ σὸν μέρος—50b), and whether he will try to do it 'so far as you are able' (καθ' ὅσον δύνασαι—51a). The importance of those phrases is not just the recognition of the almost total inability a single individual has, and by a single act, to destroy the laws, but also the bearing which they can be shown to have on the question whether the dialogue's thesis that lawbreaking is law-destruction is to be interpreted consequentially or not. This will be explained below.

From what has so far been said it can be seen how very weak the argument from consequences is against the would-be lawbreaker. Basically, it is a 'consider the consequences of your action' or 'think what will happen if you do it' argument. And basically it is a very weak argument, because in almost all circumstances the correct answer will be that very little, or even that nothing, will happen if he does it—i.e. that nothing will happen that could correctly be described both as being a consequence of his action and also as being destructive of the law. It would be quite irrational for a man who goes in for lawbreaking to be moved by the suggestion that a consequence of his lawbreaking would be a collapse in the law's efficacy, or even a diminution of it—unless he happened to be such a person, or to be in such a position, that his conduct would directly or indirectly encourage others to become lawbreakers, too; and very few lawbreakers are such persons, or are in such a position. A man who has any hope or belief that, by his own illegality, he might bring down the laws on his own, might not be certifiably insane, but he would hardly serve as a model of rationality. His only hope would lie in encouraging, by example or whatever means, others to follow his lead: and success stories of that kind must be few and far between. So, if the laws had been charging Socrates that he was proposing to act in a way that would have as a consequence, however indirect, the downfall, or the risk of downfall, of Athenian law, he could appropriately have replied that they need not worry, for there was not the slightest chance of that happening. That is a perfectly correct answer to give, if the thesis is propounded in that consequentialist form. If the objection made to my acting in a certain way is that it will produce, or is liable to produce, consequences of a certain kind, then, if it is not true that it will, or is liable to, produce those consequences, the objection collapses. If there is a valid objection to my acting that way, it will have to be different from that.

Nor is an argument of the consequential type in much better shape, if the focus is shifted from the single individual, such as Socrates, to people in general. We ask the individual then to consider, not 'Think what will happen if you do it', but 'Think what will happen if people in general do it', or in the extreme case 'Think what will happen if everybody does it'. Our conclusion will be that the man has two lines of rebuttal: (a) 'Don't worry, they won't do it'; (b) 'Even if they do, it won't have the consequences you predict'. If either one of those lines of rebuttal is sound, the generalised consequential argument against his lawbreaking fails. And (c), furthermore, he can reply that, if the generalised consequential argument is *purely* a consequential argument (in fact, as used, it seldom is), it is irrelevant to his case. It would be relevant only if the lawbreaking conduct of people in general, or of everybody (in the extreme case) were itself a consequence of his conduct. But *ex hypothesi* it is not, on this generalised consequential argument. If their conduct were a consequence of his, we should be back with the argument in its first form, and with his line of rebuttal to that.

Those answers are worth some notice on their own. To take (c) first, the argument that it must be wrong for *somebody* to do a certain thing, if it would be wrong for *everybody*, or even people in general, to do it is a badly fallacious one, and is made no more respectable by the fact that it is frequently used by parents and teachers, sincerely convinced that it is a crusher. (Some of them, knowing a little Kant, may think that they have him behind them, but they do not.) For example, the consequences of *everybody* in a given town becoming hopelessly intoxicated on the same evening would be calamitous: drunk ambulance drivers wildly trying to reach the drunk victims of car smashes caused by drunk driving, and then to deliver them into the hands of the hospital's accident staff for them drunkenly to attempt emergency operations would be just one thread of the dreadful tangle. Clearly the consequences of such generalised drunkenness would be bad enough to make it wrong for people in general, let alone everybody, to get drunk on that evening. But from that alone nothing whatever follows as to whether it would be wrong for somebody (some one person) to get drunk that evening. Whether bad consequences will follow from his drunkenness depends entirely on what he does while drunk. His driving a heavy goods vehicle on the highway or a high-speed train on the railway while in that condition is one thing; his falling into a solitary stupor in front of the late-night movie on his television set is another. To repeat: if the argument is being made one purely from consequences, then it has to be from the consequences of the conduct of the person, or persons, being talked about. From the consequences of universal, or general, drunkenness nothing can be inferred about the consequences of one person's drunkenness. Similarly in the case of lawbreaking. We might concede that in the case of a particular law (not necessarily of each particular law), and even more readily in the case of laws in general, the consequences of everybody breaking it or them would be socially undesirable or worse, and therefore that it would be wrong for everybody to do that. But we cannot, from that alone, conclude that it must be wrong for somebody (e.g. Socrates) to do it.

Even without (c), the answers in (a) and (b) are, in situations where they are true, sufficient to rebut the generalised form of the argument from consequences. That is, (a), even if we allowed that consideration of what the consequences would be if everybody, or most people, behaved in a certain way, e.g. broke a certain law, was relevant to the question whether it was wrong for a particular person to behave that way, we should have to admit that *cadit quaestio* if in fact people would not behave that way. We do not have to worry about the appalling consequences that would follow from everybody in a community getting drunk tonight, if there is not the slightest chance that they will; and we could not use the imagined appalling consequences as an argument against the single individual—as long as we continue to argue from consequences alone. Even if he conceded that the consequences of general drunkenness, or in the case of Socrates general breaking of a law, or even of the law in general, were relevant to the question whether it would be wrong for *him* to get drunk or break the law, he could reply that the argument fails, because in fact people are not all going to get drunk or break the law. *He* is the one who is going to, while others carry on as before. An activity, getting drunk, breaking the law or whatever, can be objected to on the basis of its consequences only if the activity is actually engaged in; for, if it is not engaged in, it cannot have consequences. Similarly with (b). The activity in question, to be objected to, must both *occur* and *have* the consequences. (a) was the situation in which it was denied that the activity would occur; (b) is the situation in which it is, say, conceded that the activity would occur but denied that it would have the alleged consequences. If either denial is correct, then the force of 'Think what will happen, or what the consequences will be, if everybody does that—or if people in general do that' disappears. The appearance of plausibility which the argument from consequences has derives from the fact that another and much better argument, which might be called the argument from fairness, is sometimes stated in a way which makes it look to be an argument from consequences, when in fact it is not. As will be explained later, there is a crucial difference between the two arguments. The fact that a certain kind of activity, e.g. generalised lawbreaking, which would be wrong because its consequences are bad, is *not* being engaged in is, as we have seen, a fatal objection to the argument from consequences. In the case of the argument from fairness, on the other hand, it is an essential part of the argument itself. Two arguments cannot be the same, if what is integral to one destroys the other.

There is one further weapon which a would-be lawbreaker could use against the consequentialists, a weapon taken from their own armoury. If they concede, as realism demands that they should, that the bad consequences, i.e. bad effects on the law, of his breaking it alone would be nil, but claim that the bad consequences of everybody, or of a substantial number, breaking it would be considerable, then a question about maximum utility can be asked. If the conduct of one man has no deleterious effect on the law, but the same conduct by many more has that effect, then where is the threshold? When does the bad effect begin to appear? Let us suppose, for the sake of illustration, that it begins to appear when more than 5 per cent of the population break the law, but that up to that 5 per cent no bad effect is produced. In that case, the maximum benefit of adherence to the law would be achieved, not when nobody was breaking it, but when some were successfully breaking it, as long as the total number of lawbreakers reached but did not exceed the critical 5 per cent. This would be the condition of maximum benefit, because everybody would have the advantage of there being 100 per cent conformity to the law (100 per cent here being, in realistic terms, indistinguishable from the actual 95 per cent), and in addition there would be the advantage which the 5 per cent who were successful lawbreakers gained by their being lawbreakers. The 95 per cent lawabiders have the advantage of living in a society in which 100 per cent are abiding by the law (even though only 95 per cent are in fact abiding by it). The 5 per cent lawbreakers have that advantage, plus whatever additional advantage they gain themselves by successfully breaking it. Therefore, if the case against lawbreaking rested on its consequences, and if (as seems reasonable to suppose) the bad consequences for the law do not appear with the first case of lawbreaking, we ought to want as much lawbreaking as could be absorbed without producing any bad consequences. The argument from consequences emerges as a dismally weak affair, if it is addressed to the individual person, such as Socrates—unless he happens to be a person whose conduct will influence the conduct and attitude of others in the same direction. How difficult it is nowadays to be such a person has been well illustrated by the fate of President Nixon. After America finally brought itself to acknowledge the criminality of his entourage's conduct there has been little sign of imitative movements. Watergate may have produced a slump in the reputation of lawyers (although there is little evidence even of that), but it has not harmed the law at all. The argument from consequences can begin to bite only when it is applied to, or addressed to, a substantial number of lawbreakers or would-be lawbreakers.

As mentioned at the outset, the objection to a man's breaking the law, or to people in general breaking it, based on the alleged consequences of such lawbreaking, is causal in form, and therefore borne out or not borne out, as the case may be, by the empirical facts, by what effects actually are produced by the lawbreaking. But for the objection to *be* an objection it is not sufficient that the consequences be produced, it is also required that they be bad consequences. Now, if the consequences in question are the destruction of law, it may seem so obviously true that they are bad consequences that no further discussion can be called for. If the rule of law, in some form or other, is essential to the maintenance and stability of society, how can the destruction of law be anything other than bad? Yet it is not as simple as that. It makes a difference whether we are talking about having a system of law at all, or about the particular system which, say, we do have, or about a particular law which is one of the elements of that system. A society which had no system of law at all, i.e. one in which its existing system had collapsed and had not been replaced by another would be in a bad way, indeed could not be said to be a society at all. But whether the destruction of its particular system, judged on its own, was a bad thing would depend on a number of factors, such as the quality of the system, how and in what circumstances it was destroyed, how it was replaced by another system, the quality of that system, etc. And that destruction of laws is not always bad becomes even clearer when one considers the case of particular laws. Every time that a law is repealed it is destroyed; every time that a law is allowed to lapse (in jurisdictions which recognise desuetude) it is destroyed; yet it can hardly be denied that some repeals and some lapsings represent an improvement. So, some laws are better destroyed. And the objection to destroying them by breaking them could not be that breaking them is wrong because it destroys them, but would have to be that breaking them is the wrong way of destroying them. That is the argument that it is wrong to take the law into one's own hands: if a law is to be killed, it should be killed by whatever method constitutional law provides. But, while that argument represents a generally wise and salutary policy, it is not unexceptionable. First, it will not work where the law in question is itself part of the constitutional law of repeal; and secondly, it falls foul again of the empirical facts—that sometimes a law is killed by unconstitutional means, that nobody is any the worse for it, and that the legal system is none the worse for it. It is sometimes said that a law is no good if it cannot be enforced. While that is an overstatement, it is an overstatement of a truth, viz. that a law is no good if it is not observed, and is either not enforced or not enforceable. It can happen that, due to changing social or economic conditions, a law becomes no longer appropriate; nobody bothers with it any more, and neither police nor courts do anything to enforce it; it may not have been formally pronounced dead, but it is dead. And sometimes, perhaps through insufficiently attentive legislation, a measure can get enacted which is just too silly to take seriously; the best fate for it is death by ridicule, which does nothing to injure the health of the rest of the law.

There is little doubt that, if the laws of Athens in their address to Socrates are using the argument from consequences against him, they escape using it in its crude forms. It is not suggested that what he might do will in fact, directly or indirectly, bring about the downfall of the legal system, or of any of the laws in it. Their reproach is more carefully worded—that, as the would-be escaper, Socrates is *trying* to destroy the laws; this is repeated several times, the word employed being usually ἐπιχειρεῖν, 'to put one's hand to' (cf. 50d, 51a, 52c). The charge against him does not rest on the presupposition that he is going to succeed; merely to try, to the best of his ability, will be enough. Yet, the argument might still be one of the consequence-type; and, if it is, could easily be countered by somebody in Socrates' position, by pointing out that, if there is no chance of succeeding, then trying, while it may be a waste of time, does no harm. Such an answer seems somehow to miss the point of blaming or criticising someone for trying to produce a state of affairs which is bad; and yet it only does not miss the point if the blame or criticism does not look to the consequences of successful trying. There is commonly some vacillation between two points of view in our criticising a person for trying to do something, where what he was trying to do was wrong or prohibited. This is well illustrated by the condition of modern law on criminal attempt, which is a condition by no means satisfactory to moral judgment. Commonly, in addition to substantive offences (e.g., murder, arson, rape), there are offences of attempt (e.g., attempted murder, attempted arson, attempted rape). And, of course, criminal attempts must be failures: a charge of attempted *x* can lie against an accused person only if the attempt has been unsuccessful; had it been successful, he would have been charged with the substantive offence of *x*. Given that attempts must be failures, it may seem only commonsense that in crime attempts should be treated as lesser offences, and carry lesser punishments, as they do, than the corresponding substantive offences. But is it, in fact, commonsense that a man should be punished less for an unsuccessful attempt at murdering somebody than for actually murdering him? If the object of punishing a man for what he has done is to deter him from doing such a thing again, and, through whatever publicity his case receives, similarly to deter others, then attempts should not receive lesser punishments than substantive crimes. It is not the case that a lesser punishment in prospect is needed to head a man off from committing attempted (i.e. unsuccessful) murder than is needed to head him off from committing murder, for the simple reason that nobody ever sets out to commit attempted murder. A man may say that he is going to try to kill B, but he is not using 'try' there synonymously with legal 'attempt'; in trying to kill B his intention or his hope is not, in trying, to fail to kill him, but to succeed in killing him. And what he means by saying that he is going to try to kill B is that he is going to kill him, if he can.

Again, if punishment is tied more closely to desert than it is on a purely deterrent view, the agent who has tried but failed to kill has not shown himself to be a less bad man than the one who has tried and succeeded. He has not; his intention was exactly the same, and the only difference is that in the execution of it he was more incompetent, or less fortunate, or more frustrated. So, one man may be punished less than another, not because he was less wicked, villainous or malevolent in his intentions, but because he was just luckier in that he failed. Commonly the defence offered for prescribing lesser punishment for attempts than for the substantive crimes is, first, that in the former case less harm was done: the victim was not actually raped, nor killed, nor did she have her house set on fire; and, secondly, that it provides some incentive, if the circumstances allow it, to stop before it is too late: the agent would have nothing to gain by changing his mind in the course of his effort, or by refraining from firing a second shot if the first one missed, if he risked being punished as much anyway for giving up the attempt or for failing as for succeeding.[1] There is good sense in that—given that attention is concentrated on actual or likely consequences; and it fits, or seems to fit, the principle that the law punishes only for what we actually do (including acts of omission). The consequences of unsuccessful crime are less harmful than those of successful crime; and the likely consequences will be better if a man changes his mind while engaged in committing what would be a crime, or if he does not try to do it again when his first attempt has failed. But the matter is not in law as neat and simple as that, because, in addition to the *actus reus*, there has to be the element of *mens rea*: as already mentioned, the intention in the action which ends up as an attempt is the same as the intention in the action which ends up as a substantive crime—they differ only in their outcomes, and possibly also in their circumstances. We can say that the law is interested in punishing attempts, because they are tryings which, as it turned out, were unsuccessful, but which *might have been* successful. But there are at least three might-have-beens, and of these one is an extremely Pickwickian one.

(i) If A, intending to kill B, fires a shot at him but misses, or hits him in a non-vital place, we can say that the shot might have killed B—if only A had fired straighter, or aimed better, or B had not moved so quickly, it would have killed him. A tried to kill B, and came very close to doing it. He would be guilty of attempted murder.

(ii) If A, intending to kill B, aims a loaded gun at him, but his arm is knocked aside before he fires, or he is overpowered just before he can fire, we can again say that he might have killed B. But it is not quite like the first case. There his action was completed, but did not come off. This time his action was interfered with, aborted, before it could be completed. He tried to kill B as before, but, if he came close to doing it, it was not coming close in the same way. This time he had not quite finished what he was doing when somebody else intervened. But, what we mean by saying that he might have killed B cannot be that, if he had not been prevented, he would have done

[1] In England by the Criminal Law Act 1967 s. 7 (2) an attempt is now punishable to the same extent as the substantive offence. In the U.S.A. a similar provision is contained in the Model Penal Code section 5.05.

it; for, even if not prevented, he might still have failed as in (i). In both cases, at the end there had been a risk of A killing B, in both cases there was a trying which failed, but at the time of failure in (ii) there was a risk of success, at the time of failure in (i) there was not. In (ii), as in (i), A would be guilty of attempted murder.

(iii) If A, intending to kill B, fires a shot at him and does not miss, but does no harm, because he had filled his gun with blank cartridges, mistaking them (perhaps snatching them up in the dark) for live cartridges, he again would be guilty of attempted murder. In this kind of case there is an actual impossibility of success which is not there in the other two, but it is not a bar to conviction for attempt. What is attempted may be impossible, because it cannot be done *that way* (using the wrong or inadequate means or instruments), or because it cannot be done *at all* (e.g., stealing money from a pocket which has none in it; or deceiving a man into parting with his money by making a false representation to him about something on which he knows the truth). If such cases are might-have-beens, they are very different from either of the other two. In cases of this third kind, there is no risk at all of the harm which the agent intends being produced. Yet they are punished in just the same way. Should they be? and if so, why?

The answers to these questions will bring us back to the laws' charge against Socrates. And it needs to be taken in conjunction with noticing an ambiguity in the notion of action or doing, which appears in legal thinking. Not that it is peculiar to legal thinking: it is indeed a reflection of a feature of our language, that some verbs have their outcome built into their meaning, while others do not. Thus, 'kill', 'wound', 'win', 'defeat' do, while 'attack', 'hit', 'compete', 'contend with' do not. Suppose, for example, that A, intending to kill B by poisoning, pours a fatal dose of poison into B's glass of wine, which B then drinks and so dies; and suppose that another individual, A_1, intending to kill another individual, B_1, by poisoning, pours a fatal dose of poison into B_1's glass of wine, which B_1 then does not drink, and so does not die. The only difference between the two cases lies in the conduct of B and B_1. A and A_1 did exactly the same thing—they poured poison into their victim's wine, intending that they should die from drinking it. And yet A did something which A_1 did not do—he killed his man; his action was a case of killing, and the other not, because his had an outcome which the other did not have. So, A would be guilty of murder, A_1 of attempted murder. But that A_1's offence was lesser than A's was no credit to him. He did exactly what A did, and it was just lucky for him that B_1's part in the proceedings was different from B's.

There is something morally unsatisfactory, if punishment is being handed out at all, about one man receiving a lighter punishment than a second, just because the harm actually produced by his conduct is, through circumstances which in no way reduce the culpability of his conduct, less than that produced by the other man's—and especially so when what each has contributed to the outcome is absolutely identical. On the other hand, if the law were concerned consistently only with what we do, in the sense of 'do' which refers only to the outcome of our actions, then there would be no justification for punishing at all the man whose action has no chance of producing the consequences at which it was aimed. But, in fact, the law does not concern itself, or consistently concern itself, with what we do, in that sense of the word. This is where it leans in the direction of the other element in a criminal offence, that of *mens rea* (except for strict liability offences, from which it is formally excluded). The notion of *mens rea* has been found notoriously difficult to define, but it will suffice, for the purpose of leading back to the case of Socrates in the *Crito*, if it is taken as a disjunction of the elements of intention, foresight and recklessness; in other contexts the further element of negligence would have to be taken into account also. A man shows *mens rea* in his conduct if what he intends or aims at is wrong, or if the outcome which he foresees is wrong, or if he consciously disregards the wrong which his conduct strongly risks producing. The man who tries but fails to kill displays just the same criminal intent as if he had tried and succeeded. If talk of fault, blame and responsibility is proper at all, the man who tries but fails rates the same moral assessment as the man who tries but does not fail, where what each is trying to do is the same. We do pass moral judgment on people for what they try to do and, provided that we are satisfied that they were seriously trying, our judgment on them is unmodified by the fact that they did not succeed, even by the fact that there was never any serious chance that they would. This is the ethics of character, as advanced by Hume, and earlier by Plato. According to Hume a man's character is the proper object of moral judgment: we judge him well or ill for being the sort of person that he is. His actions are only secondary objects of judgment: we judge them as the manifestations of his character. For Plato the external conduct is an image of the inner self. And modern law, while it does not allow an accused person to be judged for his character—indeed evidence of character is admissible in court only under certain conditions—and while it insists that the question at a trial is whether he did what he is charged with having done, and that the evidence must be drawn only from the facts of the present case, yet by its requirement of a *mens rea* element it judges the accused as an agent, not as a psychological mechanism for producing acts.

This seems to be the best interpretation to put on what the laws say to Socrates when charging him with trying to destroy the laws of Athens. Their argument against him is of a non-consequential kind. They are not protesting that his conduct will actually do the laws any harm at all, let alone destroy them, nor even that there is any risk that it will. But they are protesting at his showing, by his attempt to destroy them, the sort of man that he is, a man whose attitude to the law is that of a destroyer, even whose aim is that of a destroyer. That such an aim does not have the slightest chance of success is irrelevant; what is significant is what it reveals—the character of a man who would destroy the laws, if only he could. When the laws tell Socrates that, if he escapes and makes his way to a well-governed city, he will be regarded as a 'destroyer of laws' (νόμων διαφθορεύς, 53b–c), that appears to be what they mean —a man who is willing and prepared to destroy the laws. More cannot be claimed for this interpretation than that it allows one to ascribe to the personified laws of Athens the most reasonable view that can be found which is also consistent with the text. Some reason for hesitation is provided by the fact that in the same sentence as Socrates is called a destroyer of laws it is alleged that he will by his conduct confirm the jury which convicted him at his trial in their assurance that they gave the correct verdict, because they will naturally suppose that anybody who was a destroyer of laws would emphatically be a destroyer of young and foolish men (53c). But he had not been tried and convicted on the charge of performing actions which were manifestations of the character of a youth-destroyer; it had been rather that he had actually been doing some actual destroying or corrupting of actual young people (*Euth.* 2–3, *Apol.* 24). The difficulty in making such a charge stick in a well-conducted trial would be the difficulty of producing clear instances of young people who had actually been, to whatever degree, corrupted by their association with Socrates. A corresponding difficulty faces obscenity charges in England under the Obscene Publications Acts 1959 and 1964, given the statutory definition of obscenity in terms of tendency 'to deprave and corrupt' those likely to read, see or hear the matter contained in the allegedly obscene article. In any obscenity trial in which that test was rigorously interpreted, the jury would have to decide (1) what would count as corrupting (i.e. what change in a person exposed to the allegedly obscene article would count as his having been in some degree corrupted), and (2) what evidence there was (a) for the historical judgment that some such person so exposed actually had been, or actually was being, in some degree corrupted; or (b) for the subjunctive judgment that some such person would, if so exposed, be in some degree corrupted. With appropriate substitutions, decisions of the same form could properly have been demanded of the jury at Socrates' trial; it was unfortunate for him that they were not.

For some conduct there would be a third possibility (c) that the conduct complained of had a tendency to produce a certain effect, even though it would not produce it; and the idea of this possibility might lie behind some prosecutions for obscenity. An illuminating comparison can be made with poisoning a water supply, i.e. discharging into the water a poisonous substance that had a natural tendency to make the water unfit to drink; and we shall suppose that to have been made an offence of strict liability. To say that the poison has that tendency is to say that it would make the water unfit to drink in the absence of either corrective measures or natural elements or growths in the water which would counteract the poison; then the poison has the tendency to produce the effect, even though, thanks to the contrived or natural counteraction, there is no risk of its producing it. And the manager of a factory discharging chemical effluent into the river which fed the water reservoir might be charged with poisoning the water supply, although there was no danger of the water being made unfit to drink, and even though there was no question of negligence nor of criminal attempt. Similarly, some publications might be alleged to have a tendency to corrupt, even though there was, in fact, due to whatever counteracting influences, no danger of anyone being actually corrupted; and Socrates might be alleged to be a destroyer of youth in that sense, that his conduct and conversation had a natural tendency to corrupt youth, even though, in fact, thanks to fine character building by education at home and in school, there was no danger of any young person actually being destroyed by him. This charge would not require that he was *trying* to corrupt youth.

That thesis, however, is less difficult to make out in the case of poisoning water than in those of corrupting minds or destroying youth, because an epistemic condition can be more easily met for it than for them—given that the water has not actually been made unfit to drink, and that in the other cases nobody has actually been corrupted and destroyed. In the case of the poison it can readily be established by chemical analysis and experiment what the effects of the water would be, if the counteractive factors, which are present, had been absent. But to establish the corresponding thing in the other cases, where what would be affected is a person's mind or character, would be vastly more difficult, not only because of the moral objection to conducting the necessary experiments, but also because, even if they could be allowed to be conducted, people are greatly more complex than water, people differ from each other in many more various ways than samples of water, and the task of reliably confirming or disconfirming such a sociological hypothesis would demand extraordinary resources.

Socrates' jury could have considered whether he had been destroying youth in *that* sense, and, in the absence of strict requirements of evidence and legal proof, might have satisfied themselves that he had been. But the *Euthyphro* passage tells against it: it suggests that his alleged offence was actually to have destroyed some young people. A man can have poisoned the water without having made it poisonous to drink, but he cannot have destroyed any young people, unless some young people have been destroyed. So they had not regarded him either as a man whose conduct had a tendency to destroy youth or as one who would destroy youth if he could (the latter requires trying to destroy, the former does not); and therefore their finding against him would not be exactly analogous to the case of the laws against him in the *Crito*. Yet the single phrase-form 'destroyer of ——' would not be inappropriate in either case; and therefore we can still be left with the view that the laws were charging Socrates with being one who, by escaping from prison, shows himself a man who would destroy the laws, if he could; that action is the action of such a man, whether or not it has, or has any prospect of having, such an outcome; it is the action of such a man *trying* to destroy the laws. So, the complaint against him is not his conduct itself— the actions of which it consists will be harmless and ineffective, in relation to the law—but the character, attitude and aims which it expresses; and judgment on them has nothing to do with success or failure in execution.

Whether or not Plato, at the time of writing the *Crito*, was aware of the unsatisfactoriness of treating attempted and successful offences differently, and also the unsatisfactoriness of treating them alike, he certainly appreciated the problem later, for he explicitly dealt with it in the *Laws* (877). A citizen who wounds another citizen with intent to kill (Plato does not deal with the case where in the attempt to kill no injury is inflicted at all) should be treated with no more respect than a killer, and indeed should be made to stand trial for murder. On the other hand, after conviction the punishment awarded should respect both the fact that things did not turn out entirely for the worst and the accused's guardian spirit who was responsible for the fact that they did not; instead of receiving the death penalty, the man was to suffer lifelong banishment and to compensate the victim for whatever injury he had suffered. If it was a case of husband wounding wife (or *vice versa*) with intent to kill, the punishment again was to be lifelong banishment. But, if it was a child wounding a parent in attempt to kill, or a slave a master or one sibling another, then the penalty was to be death. In other words, if a man was tried for having performed an act of wounding with specific intent, the intent being to kill, the charge against him was to be the same as if the intent had been successfully executed, and the conviction was to be for murder, even though the victim was not dead; there should be no distinction between the stigma of conviction for murder and that for attempted murder. In the case of blood relatives (nothing is said about parent attempting to kill child), and of slave attempting to kill master, the punishments for the attempted and the substantive crimes were to be the same, presumably because by committing a crime of such an unspeakable kind (the relationship involved being what it was) the offender showed himself to be beyond cure (cf. 854e). But in other cases punishment for the attempt was to be somewhat lighter—only because the assailant had been fortunate enough not to have succeeded, and not to have been abandoned by his guardian spirit. For Plato, the purpose of punishment was twofold: making good to the victim the damage actually suffered, and encouragement to the offender to reform (933e). Nowadays, without the benefit of a family or personal genius to guide us back to the path of virtue (cf. *Phaedo* 107d), we have a harder task in reconciling the two sides of the law of attempt.

There is some contrast between a strictly moral viewpoint and a strictly legal viewpoint on people's activities. Let us continue with the example of obscenity. If the story sometimes told by the publisher or seller of an article, alleged by critics or prosecution to be obscene, is true, it was not part of his intention to corrupt the young or anybody else; his intention was solely to make as good a living as he could out of meeting that particular market demand. In law that probably would not be admissible in defence, because for obscenity offences the *mens rea* requirement appears to be minimal, if necessary at all. However, nobody sells pornography with his eyes closed, and, whether or not he believes that there is any risk that what he sells will deprave and corrupt some of those who see it, he is not going to be believed if he denies that he was aware that others might think there was such a risk, or that he was untroubled by that. So, even if not technically reckless, he was untroubled by the thought of a risk, or insufficiently troubled to be diverted from his activities. Most people would find it very hard to take the word of a seller of pornography who protested that he would get out of the business tomorrow if he thought for a moment that there was any chance of anybody being harmed by his wares; we are all going to think that he could not care less what might happen to his readers. Because, by engaging in that trade, he shows himself to be the sort of man that he is, we find it very easy to condemn him morally, and also to approve of his conviction in the local court after the police have raided his premises and he has been brought to trial; he only got what he deserved. But should it be so easy to approve of his conviction? It may be all right to condemn him as a man on the basis of his activities, but that is not the business of the law. Under the law of obscenity we ought not to have any sympathy with a man's conviction, however vile and despicable he may be, unless there actually was some risk of corrupting some of the people. The law's business is with what we do, and risk doing, to each other. In terms only of depraving, the law should tolerate the depraver and his activities as long as he does not deprave; even more strongly, it should tolerate his trying to deprave, as long as there is no chance of his succeeding. The depraver who has no chance at all of depraving is an objectionable but also a harmless member of society. If the law goes after him (as in effect it does), if the corrupting influence of his wares is not established, it will have to be like the White Queen, and defend the practices of punishing *before* the crime is committed. Of course, there are other reasons why the law cannot leave him alone, if it accepts that some published material really can tend to deprave and corrupt. First, given that there are profits to be made out of the activity (and there any correspondence with the case of Socrates immediately breaks down), others may be encouraged by his non-prosecution to copy him, and of them some may be more efficient than he at depraving and corrupting. Again the law just does not have time to attempt a discrimination between potentially unsuccessful and potentially successful depravers; and that is easier to accept when *moral* justice does not demand that it should. But at least it ought to determine that the accused is a member of a class (publishers of material of a certain description), of whom it is typical that they tend to deprave and corrupt. Similar considerations ought, in natural justice, to have applied to the trial of Socrates on the charge of corrupting youth. That they were not applied, and that it does not seem to have been thought that they should have been, is probably a reflection of the generally accepted view that a man had no human rights which it was the business of the courts to protect, and that in a trial for a public offence the interest of public security or good was the only one of importance.

But, even if there is some injustice in the law actually prosecuting a man for being a corrupter, in the absence of any evidence that what he was doing was corrupting anybody, or coming within any likelihood of doing it, the same kind of restriction does not seem to bind what we might call moral prosecution. The moral judgments to be made about people are not all for particular things they have done, or tried to do. If there is evidence available that a man is the sort of man to do, or to try to do, something, where that something is objectionable by way of intention, effects, or both, then we do not find it wrong to judge him as a man of that sort, even if he has not yet tried to do a thing of that kind. We must, indeed, have some of his acts and utterances to go on, for otherwise we would have no evidence at all of his attitude and character. But we do not have to wait for him even to begin the performance of an act of a certain kind before we can justifiably charge him with being a man who would perform acts of that kind. The charge which the laws bring against Socrates is not a legal complaint that anything he has done or might do would destroy, or go anywhere near destroying, the laws, but is a moral complaint that he is a law-destroyer, the sort of man who would destroy the laws if he could; and clear evidence that he is would be his participation in the lawbreaking plot to effect a gaol-break for him before his execution could be carried out. In fact, the complaint of the laws against Socrates goes further than that. Participation in an escape from prison not only will be evidence that he is a law-destroyer, it will be an act expressing his intention to destroy the law, so far as he is able, it will be an actual manifestation of his character as a law-destroyer, of his attitude to law-destruction; all that could be, without his conduct having the slightest tendency to destroy the laws. What we might not be able to judge him for in a legal court we could judge him for in a moral court.

It does seem suitable that I should be open to criticism, not merely for what I do, but also for the intention with which I do it, even where there is no chance of fulfilling that intention, and further for being the sort of person to do such a thing, even if I have not yet done it, nor even tried to. The kind of criticism to be made of conduct and character respectively may be different, but each alike is moral criticism.

What is involved in the laws' criticism of Socrates as an escaper, if the suggested interpretation is accepted, is the truth that there can be people in society about whom nothing should be done, for they are unable to achieve any harm, but who are justifiably deplored, because of the kind of people that they are and of the attitudes which their conduct and utterances express. Actual examples from our own times are not hard to bring to mind, but the laws of libel make it prudent not to name them. They flourish in the seamier pockets of business, and they can be found by uncovering the dirty undersides of some of the stones of politics. Nor do they have to be on the make for themselves; there is, for instance, the trade union leader of a certain kind, who not merely says that it is his job to consider the interests only of his members, but who expresses sneering disregard and contempt for the helpless public affected by the strike. They are all misanthropes of one sort or another, and they come across as people whom society would be much more agreeable without. They are poisonous and odious, but if they are, as many are, seedy small-time operators, unsuccessful in their ploys of exploitation, they do not actually manage to poison the social stream. For this reason one must treat with scepticism the sentiments, wholly sincere though they are, of an author who can write of a certain kind of criminal that he 'is no menace to others, but he does threaten one of the great principles upon which society is based'.[1] What can it be to threaten such a principle, if not to act in a way which introduces, or increases, a risk that the principle will become less effective in the society, i.e. will be less adhered to, respected, applied or enforced? A man whose conduct will not introduce or increase such a risk cannot, in any serious sense, be said to threaten the principle. If he were more powerful, or there were

---

[1] Patrick Devlin, *The Enforcement of Morals* (London: Oxford University Press, 1965), p. 6.

K

more like him, things might be different; but, unless so, they are not. Furthermore, if a growing practice of euthanasia (to use an example which the author had in mind) *were* to lead to a growing social acceptance of the principle of euthanasia, then it would not so much be the case that a principle was being threatened or destroyed upon which society was based, as that a new principle was at least partially replacing an old principle as basis to the society. The claim that the breach of one of society's principles 'is an offence not merely against the person who is injured but against society as a whole'[1] is a well-known claim of long tradition, but it is also a cheque that is more often flourished than cashed.

So, Socrates could be a destroyer of law without being the slightest risk or threat to the life of the law; and an enlightened system, if it knew that, would make its adverse moral judgment on him but leave him alone. But would he have to agree that in breaking the law which determined the execution of his sentence he was manifesting his character as a destroyer of law? Surely not. He would agree that man should be ruled by law, not law by man (cf. *Ep.* VIII. 354c), and he could agree that there would be good contractual reasons that he should accept the application of the law making court decision binding, but he would not have thereby to agree that a man who was not prepared to accept the application of that law was manifesting the character of a law-destroyer. That a man has agreed to a law giving binding force to the rulings of the law's officials may be a good reason for his accepting those rulings, and for characterising him as a law-destroyer if he does not, but it is not an overwhelmingly good reason. It is a very good reason, if the officials are seen to be making their rulings fairly and conscientiously in accordance with the rules of the system, in Socrates' case in accordance with the substantive and procedural law of the criminal code; but it is a less good reason, if they are not. And, although it may be some consolation to a convicted person to know that he has been wronged not by the laws but by men (54b–c), consolation may not meet the case. He may believe that the best way to frustrate or protest the misapplication of a good law, or the implementation of a bad

---

[1] Ibid., p. 7.

law, is to take the matter into his own hands. He may then be open to criticism for error of judgment, he may be faulted for assuming an improper role, but he can hardly be told that his attitude is that of a law-destroyer. In fact, however misguided or blameworthy he may be in his conduct, his attitude is the exact opposite: he sees himself as a champion of law, against its perversion by legislators or by officials of the judicial system. His conduct could, in the unlikely event of his being a powerful enough single influence, have the consequence of destroying the laws, but he could not properly be accused of *trying* to destroy them. We do not have to accept the point of what he is trying to do, but we do have to see it.

Finally, it is interesting to note that what would now commend itself to many as one of the strongest reasons, if not the strongest, for obedience to law would hardly have been intelligible to Socrates and his contemporaries, viz. the unfairness to others of one's disobedience; it is an indication how much thinking on this topic has changed, especially recently. Although the principle of not wronging others, not treating them unjustly, is the fundamental principle of the *Crito*, on which stands each of the three arguments against disobedience to law, it is nowhere suggested, either by Socrates or by the personified laws of Athens, that to break the law is to treat other *people* unjustly. The idea that the duty to refrain from lawbreaking flowed from a relationship between subject and ruler (the ruler being, not the government of the day, but that whose authority a legitimate government carried—specified in the *Crito* variously as the city, the state, the laws themselves) was what Socrates was arguing. The idea that the duty might flow from a relationship between subject and fellow subjects never seems to have occurred to him; nor would he have found it easier to accept than the notion of human rights, from which it derives. And yet in any case in which it is wrong to break the law part and in many cases the whole of the wrongness of the lawbreaking lies in its unfairness to others who are keeping the law and expecting it to be kept. In particular offences of some kinds the factor of unfairness is such a minimal element of the wrongness that it can seem inappropriate even to mention it; in others it may be all the wrongness that there is.

The general principle of the argument that it is unfair to others to break a law which they are keeping is that the law-breaker gains the advantage which they all do from the fact of the law's generally successful operation (which will include both the value of its aim being even partially achieved, e.g. some improvement of security of life, and the value of its being generally observed and expected to be observed), while at the same time he gains that further advantage of breaking the law which others are forgoing by keeping it; further, not only does he get a double advantage, but he gets it by a means which is unfair to the others. He profits from the operation of a law which serves a useful social purpose, both by the benefit which (in the case of a good law) it promotes and by its receiving general conformity; and he further profits by not himself paying the price of obedience, which may be inconvenient and expensive for those who do pay it. A paradigm case is that of the freeloader or cheat who gets the benefits of a taxing system without paying his share of the dues, where the dues are needed to provide the benefits. That this is a paradigm case tends to be obscured by the fact that so few of us behave as if it were: we think nothing of finding every way we can of avoiding taxes. In a modern capitalist economy the 'benefits' secured by tax collection are largely remote, indirect and even questionable, while the great disparities of individual wealth and income mean that the pattern of distribution of benefits does not match the pattern of collection of taxes. It is quite right that it does not, but it makes it all the easier to think of others as 'them' instead of as 'us'.

If, with regard to some laws, we ask why it is, or would be, wrong to break them, a sufficient answer can be provided by citing the wrong which they prohibit. What is wrong with committing legal offences of a generally harmful or damaging kind is that the conduct constituting the offence, e.g. violence to the person or to property, is itself morally objectionable; and it would be wrong to behave that way even in the absence of legal prohibition. Is it also wrong, because unfair or unjust, to gain the advantage of another keeping the law and expecting one to do the same, plus the advantage of not keeping it one-self in that situation? Is the mugger treating his victim (and others) unfairly by mugging an individual who is neither trying to commit a mugging himself nor expecting others to mug him? If under law men have a duty to others not to attack them, then a person has a legal right not to be attacked, plus any other legal rights conferred and supposedly protected by any other related laws. In general, in a modern western society an individual has the legal right to go about his own lawful pursuits peaceably and unmolested, and the legal duty not to prevent, nor to interfere with, others doing the same. The efficacy of the legal system and its consequential benefits to those living under it is determined by the reliability of the expectations which it encourages in them. So, a man who gains an end by using illegal means which others, having similar ends, feel inhibited by living under law from using, gains an advantage over them, which they have a moral right that he should not try to gain in such a way. But is he, by gaining that advantage which others are forgoing and which he can expect to gain only if others (or enough others) do forgo it, being unfair to them? And, in any case, is such a consideration applicable in the case of legal offences consisting of conduct which is wrong, even apart from its being proscribed as an offence? Is the bank cashier treated unjustly by the bank robber who shoots and kills him in the course of robbing the bank? There seems no reason to deny it, although, as it is the least of the wrongs which the robber has done to him, it is inappropriate to call attention to it. But in a situation of a special type attention may have to be drawn to it. In the U.S.A., for example, where murder is a state, not a federal, offence, the only way in which federal authorities have been able to bring prosecutions against persons known to have committed murder in states where for reasons of political or racist prejudice state prosecutors either could not or would not secure convictions for murder, has been to indict on the charge of depriving the dead man of his civil rights. It is a milk-and-water charge to bring against the man who kills another for being an uppity nigra or a civil rights worker, but it is the only charge open to the federal law officers. In other, less unusual, circumstances to say that what is wrong with illegally killing to secure your ends is that you are taking advantage of others (including your victim) who refrain from illegally killing to secure theirs, is at worst false, at best to get the emphasis seriously askew. It is false, if it means that that is all that is

wrong, it misemphasises, if it suggests that it is a seriously
wrong-making element in the situation; there is enough wrong
with the killing, without bothering about its unfairness to non-
killers.

But by no means all laws calling for obedience are of that
kind. Plenty of laws, for social, economic and fiscal reasons,
require certain conduct, making the opposite conduct illegal,
where there would be nothing wrong at all with the proscribed
conduct in the absence of the law concerned. The conduct in
such a case can be called wrong only if it is describable within
the framework of the law making it an offence. While it is,
independently of law, wrong to leave a vehicle adjacent to and
blocking access to a fire hydrant, it is not, independently of
law, wrong to leave a car for two or three hours in a one-hour
parking zone. What is wrong with lawbreaking of the second
kind is less the harm it does to somebody else—and it may not
do any harm at all, e.g. if the parking zone happens not to be
congested that day—than the fact that the agent is occupying
a privileged position without having been put into, or selected
for, that position by a method which is fair to others. And that
is the heart of the unfairness argument. It is not just that the
lawbreaker is gaining an advantage which the lawabider for-
goes, but its being an advantage for him *requires* it to be an
exception to the rule, i.e. requires that others are forgoing it;
and not only does it have to be an exception but it is he who
chooses it for himself. That is what distinguishes the objection
to lawbreaking on the basis of its unfairness to others who are
keeping that law from the objection, whether in its Kantian or
its consequential form, on the basis of what it would be like if
everybody did that. To the latter the reply 'Don't worry, they
won't' is, if correct, a perfectly good answer, to the former it
does not begin to be a good answer, for what it does is simply
to bring out the point of the objection, not to respond to it.
What is wrong with the lawbreaker is not just that he is occupying a privileged position, which depends on others, or many
others, not also occupying or trying to occupy it, but that he
has secured it by an unfair method, viz. choosing himself for it.
There *may* be nothing wrong with occupying the privileged
position, if it has been secured by a method which is fair, such
as by free election or as the result of an open and equal chance

lottery. But the lawbreaker does not get into his position by such a method, or with the free consent of all the other law-abiders; he gets there by himself putting himself into it. The protest, on behalf of the others, 'Who are you to . . .?', is very much to the point.

Not all offences in which harm is done to others are such that it is out of place to object to them on the ground of their unfairness to others. Murder is such a case, and perhaps any offence involving violence to the person is, but other cases can be thought of where harm to others is done, but where also the unfairness of the agent's act of lawbreaking is a major ground for condemning it. Queue-jumping would be a good example. The man who by some illegality gets himself or a relative or a friend to the head of a housing list in front of others who have been waiting their turn harms each of them by making them wait somewhat longer for a house than they otherwise would have waited; but also—and that is what would cause the indignation if it became known—he has treated them unfairly by jumping to the head of the queue in the illegal way that he has. It should be added, however, that the unfairness to others of the lawbreaker's selecting himself for the privileged position can be mitigated or even obliterated by other factors, if present; consequently, condemnation of lawbreaking on grounds of its unfairness to others cannot be absolute. The lawbreaking act, for example, might be one undertaken as some kind of civil disobedience, as a way of protesting against bureaucratic red-tapery, and the general unsatisfactoriness of things as they are. And the act, as being of that kind, might be justified, might even be applauded by those who in particular were treated unfairly by it. The woman who in England walked into a hospital in July 1977, found an empty bed and deposited herself in it as a protest at being kept waiting so long by the National Health Service for a gallstone operation performed an act of that kind, whether or not it had any actual effect in changing admissions practice. She was allowed to stay, she got her operation, and the health authorities did some face saving by claiming that no patients ahead of her on the waiting list were made to suffer, because the operation was performed by surgeons and theatre staff in their off-duty time.

The argument that lawbreaking is wrong because unfair to

others cannot apply in all cases, for it presupposes that others are keeping the law. It is only to them that it is unfair; and consequently, it would not be unfair to them, if they too were breaking the law. Therefore, when enough people are breaking a law, either it is not wrong to break it or there will have to be some other reason for its being wrong. The first alternative is not acceptable, for it means that there is nothing wrong with breaking a law, as long as enough other people are breaking it, too. And, although there are from time to time laws which are generally broken, and which arguably there is nothing wrong in breaking, that many or most other people are breaking them cannot be the reason why there is nothing wrong with breaking them. For the principle that, whatever the law, disobedience to it is, if sufficiently general, all right does not sit well with the idea and purpose of a legal system. Therefore, the fairness argument cannot stand on its own. Nor indeed is it reasonable to expect any single argument for obedience to law to stand on its own. Socrates endorsed three distinguishable reasons why he should obey. For the rest of us it is not difficult to think of others, perhaps better than his, none perhaps uniformly pervasive through varieties of law and varieties of social situation. But on behalf of the reason of fairness it can be said that, the more a society is ruled by law, the more pervasive a reason for obedience it becomes; it reflects, in a moral way, the simple but not trivial truth that other people are people.

Translation of the *Crito*

The scene is Socrates' cell in the Athens prison on a morning in 399 B.C., where he is awaiting the carrying out of the death sentence which the court had pronounced on him a few weeks earlier, after convicting him of the offences of religious heresy and of corrupting the young. The time is shortly before dawn: Socrates is still asleep, and his old friend Crito is sitting beside the bed. He has come to visit Socrates unusually early, bearing the news that he is likely to be required to drink the fatal hemlock the following day. Crito wants to persuade him to agree to his friends arranging for him to escape from prison before it is too late. The conversation which follows is between the two men after Socrates has woken up.

43   SOCRATES: Why have you come at this hour, Crito? Or, isn't it still early?

CRITO: It certainly is.

SOCRATES: About what time is it?

CRITO: It is early light, just before dawn.

SOCRATES: I am surprised that the prison guard answered you.

CRITO: He is used to me now, Socrates, because I come and go here so often—partly too, he has had some favours from me.

SOCRATES: Have you just arrived, or have you been here for some time?

CRITO: For quite some time.

b   SOCRATES: Then why didn't you wake me immediately, instead of sitting silently beside me?

CRITO: Heavens no, Socrates. I wouldn't have chosen to be in such a sleepless and distressed state as I am—and yet I have been wondering at you, as I observed how peacefully you sleep; and I purposely didn't wake you, so that you could continue as peacefully as possible. Often indeed throughout my life have I counted you happy for your temperament, but most of all now in your present plight, for the easy and gentle way you bear it.

SOCRATES: Well indeed, Crito, it would be inappropriate for a man as old as myself to show distress if the time has now come when he must die.

c   CRITO: And yet other people of your age, Socrates, are caught in similar plights, but their age doesn't spare them from being angry at the fate which has come on them.

SOCRATES: That's true. But now why have you come so early?

CRITO: Bearing bad news, Socrates, not for you, as it seems, but for myself and for all those close to you bad news and heavy news, which I think that I would find it the heaviest to bear.

SOCRATES: What news is this? Has the vessel arrived from
d   Delos, the one whose arrival marks the time when I must die?[1]

CRITO: It hasn't arrived yet, but I think it will get here today from what is reported by some people who have come from Sunium and left it there. It is clear, then, from their news that it will get here today, and it will have to be tomorrow that you end your life.

SOCRATES: Well, with the gods' help, Crito, if this is their pleasure, let it be so. But yet I don't think the boat will come today.

44   CRITO: How do you tell that?

SOCRATES: I'll tell you. It is the day after the one when the boat arrives, I believe, that I have to die.

CRITO: Well, that's certainly what those who are in charge of these things say.

SOCRATES: Then I do not think the boat will arrive during the day which is coming on us, but on the next day. And I tell that from a dream I had a little while ago during the night. And you're likely to have been timely in not waking me.

CRITO: What then was the dream?

SOCRATES: I thought a woman approached me, who was
b   beautiful and comely, wearing white clothes, and she addressed me and said: 'Socrates, On the third day thou art to come to the rich land of Phthia.'[2]

CRITO: That was a strange dream, Socrates.

[1] In Athens the execution of a death sentence usually followed within a day of its pronouncement. But it happened that the opening of Socrates' trial coincided with the beginning of a religious mission to Delos, and that, as no executions were allowed to take place until the mission was completed with the boat's return to Athens, there was in his case a delay of several weeks between the passing of the sentence and his death.

[2] This line is almost a quotation from Homer. *Il.* ix. 363. Phthia was the home of Achilles.

SOCRATES: And yet a perfectly clear one, as it seems to me, Crito.

CRITO: Only too clear, very likely. But, my dear Socrates, even now listen to me and let yourself be saved. As for myself, if you die, it will be not one disaster only: apart from being bereft of an intimate friend, such a one as I shall never find again, I shall also appear to many people, who don't know you and me

c well, as one who was able to save you, if I had been willing to spend what it would cost, but neglected to do so. And yet what could be a more shameful reputation than that—to be thought to value money more than friends? For most people will not believe that it was you yourself who were not prepared to get away from here, although we were eager to do it.

SOCRATES: But why should we, my good Crito, care so much about popular opinion? For the most enlightened people, who are more worth considering, will believe that things have been done in just the way they have been done.

d CRITO: But surely you see, Socrates, that one has to pay attention to popular opinion. Your present predicament makes it clear enough that the people are capable of performing, not the smallest of ills, but just about the greatest, if one is discredited among them.

SOCRATES: Crito, would that the people were able to perform the greatest ills, so that they were also capable of performing the greatest goods—that would be splendid. But, as it is, they can do neither: they cannot make a man wise, and they cannot make him foolish, but they act quite haphazardly.

e CRITO: Well, let that be so. But tell me this, Socrates. You're not, I hope, concerned for me and the rest of your friends, lest, if you do escape from this place, common informers will make trouble for us for having snatched you out of here, and that we shall be required either to lose all our property or to pay heavy fines, or even to suffer something further in addition? If you do

45 have some such fear, please forget it; for we have the right to run this risk in rescuing you, indeed an even greater risk, if need be. But be advised by me, and do as I say.

SOCRATES: Yes, I am concerned about those things, Crito, and many others too.

CRITO: Then don't be afraid of it—and in any case the sum isn't great for which some people are willing to rescue you and

get you away from here. Then don't you see how cheap these
b informers are, and that it wouldn't need much money to fix
them? You already have at your disposal my money—which
will be enough, in my opinion; and furthermore, just supposing
that out of some anxiety for me you think you shouldn't spend
my money, there are these visitors to Athens who are prepared
to spend theirs. One of them has actually provided sufficient
funds for this very purpose, Simmias from Thebes, while Cebes
is ready to do it, and many others too. So, as I say, don't from
fear on that account hesitate to save yourself, and don't let what
you said in court make difficulties for you—I mean that, if you
c were to go away, you wouldn't know what to do with yourself.[1]
For, in general, there are many places where they will welcome
you if you go there; and, in particular, if you want to go to
Thessaly, I have people there who have been guests of mine,
who will esteem you very highly and will provide you with
security, so that nobody in Thessaly will cause you any trouble.

What is more, Socrates, I don't think that what you are trying
to do is right, throwing your life away when saving it is possible;
and you are striving to have the very thing happen to you for
which your enemies would strive, and indeed did strive when
they were wanting to destroy you. In addition I, at any rate,
think you are betraying your sons, whom you would go away
d and abandon, when you could bring them up and educate them
—as far as you're concerned, they will fare in whatever way they
happen to fare; but in fact, very probably, they will happen to
fare in that kind of way which does usually befall orphans after
the loss of their parents. For either one shouldn't have children,
or one should share and go through with the trouble of raising
and educating them—while you seem to me to be choosing the
easiest way out. But, whatever a man of virtue and courage
would choose that is what one should choose, at least if one
claims to have cared for virtue all one's life. For I am ashamed,
e both on your account and for us your close friends, that the whole
affair concerning you should seem to have been managed with a

---

[1] 'I know quite well that wherever I go the young will listen to me talking,
as they do here. If I keep them away from me, they would banish me (persuading their elders to do it); alternatively, if I do not keep them away, then
their fathers and family would banish me for the sake of those same young
people.' (*Apol.* 37d)

lack of courage on our part: there was the way your case came into court, when it was possible for it not to have gone into court at all, there was the way the actual course of the trial went, and lastly there is this, the crowning absurdity, that through a faint-heartedness and failure of courage of ours you appear to have

46   got away from us—we didn't save you and you didn't save yourself, when it was perfectly possible and manageable if we had been the slightest help at all. So realise, Socrates, that at the same time as the bad outcome there is the disgrace for you and us. But consider—although it's no longer the time for consider-ing, the time for that is past: there is only one thing to consider. Everything must be carried out in the course of the coming night; but, if we delay, we cannot do it, and the possibility is no longer there. All ways round, Socrates, be persuaded by me, and do as I say.

b   SOCRATES: My dear Crito, your concern for me would count for a lot if there were some truth behind it; otherwise, the greater it is, the harder it is to handle. So, we have to consider whether we must do what you recommend or not—given that this is not now for the first time the case, but that it has always been my way not to follow the call of anything else in me rather than that of reason—that is, whatever seemed to me best on reflection. Certainly the considerations which I used to declare previously

c   I cannot reject now, when this misfortune has fallen on me; they seem to me to be very much what they were, and I respect and honour the same ones as before. If we have no better ones to proclaim in the present situation, be sure that I certainly shall not agree with you, not even if the power of public opinion were to scare us like children even more than already, by visiting us with imprisonment and death and confiscation of wealth. How then are we most temperately to consider the matter? Perhaps, if we take up the argument which you give about the opinions of

d   others. Was it always well said or not that one should pay attention to some opinions, but not to others? Or was it fine to say it before the requirement that I die arose, but now it has become clear that it was said ill and for the sake of argument, and that it was really childish nonsense? I am eager to pursue this enquiry with you, Crito, in order to see whether the principle seems any different to me, given my present position, or whether it is the same, and whether we should say goodbye to it or should obey it. In my opinion something of this kind was always asserted by those who thought they had something to say, something, that is, like what I said just now, that of the opinions which men hold some should be taken seriously, and others not.

e In heaven's name, Crito, doesn't this seem to you to be well said? I ask you because you are not likely, as far as human pros-

47 pects go, to die tomorrow, and the present calamity would not distort your judgment. Now consider—does it not seem to you to be justifiably enough said that one should not respect every opinion that men express, but only some and not others—and again not every man's opinions, but only those of some and not of others? What do you say? Isn't that a fair claim?

CRITO: Yes, it is.

SOCRATES: Then the good opinions one should respect, the bad ones not?

CRITO: Yes.

SOCRATES: And are good opinions those of wise people, bad ones those of foolish people?

CRITO: How else?

SOCRATES: Well then, how well said was the following? When a man is in physical training and practising at it, does he pay

b attention to favourable and unfavourable comments and opinions from everybody, or just to those of that one individual who happens to be his physician or his trainer?

CRITO: To the latter only.

SOCRATES: Then he should fear the criticisms and welcome the praise just of that one man, and not of the many others.

CRITO: Obviously.

SOCRATES: This then is the way he must practise and train and eat and drink, whatever way seems right to the one man, the one with knowledge and expertise, rather than in the ways that seem right to all the others.

CRITO: That's so.

c SOCRATES: Well then. If he doesn't obey the one man, and shows no respect for his opinion and his praise, but listens to what is said by the many who have no expert knowledge, will he not come to some harm?

CRITO: How can he avoid it?

SOCRATES: What is the harm, and where does it aim—at what part of the disobedient person?

CRITO: Obviously at his body; for that is what is being ruined.

SOCRATES: You're right. Then are the rest of things like that, Crito—to save us going through them all individually? Especially concerning the just and the unjust, fine and shameful, good and bad, about which we are deliberating—should we follow the opinion of the many and fear that? Or should we go by the opinion of the one man, if there is such a man with expert knowledge, before whom we should feel shame and fear more than before all the others taken together? If we don't follow him, we shall destroy and mutilate that part of us which is improved by right conduct and ruined by ill conduct. Isn't that so?

CRITO: I certainly think so, Socrates.

SOCRATES: Well then, if we take that part of us which is improved by healthy living and corrupted by unhealthy living, and if we ruin it by not adhering to the opinion of those who really know, is life worth living for us with that part corrupted? And that part of us is our body. Isn't that so?

CRITO: Yes.

SOCRATES: Then is our life worth living with a body that is in bad condition and corrupted?

CRITO: No way.

SOCRATES: But is our life worth living with that part of us corrupted, where what is *morally wrong* mutilates, and what is *right* benefits? Or do we think to be less important than the body that part of us, whatever it is in us, with which right and wrong are concerned?

CRITO: Certainly not.

SOCRATES: Instead it is more valuable?

CRITO: Yes, much.

SOCRATES: In that case, good sir, we should not at all take into account here what most people will say about us, but only what the man says who knows about right and wrong—I mean the one man and the real truth. So, in the first place, you are not making a correct proposal here, when you propose that we must take into account popular opinion about the right, the fine and the good and their opposites. 'And yet,' somebody might say, 'the people do have the capability of putting us to death.'

CRITO: Indeed, that's clear—for it would be said, Socrates. You're right.

SOCRATES: But, dear friend, this line of argument which we

have just been through seems to me to be still just as it was before. And this in turn is what you must examine to see if it still holds good for us or not, namely that it is not living but living well that is to be most highly prized.

CRITO: But it does hold.

SOCRATES: And the proposition that living well is identical with living honourably and justly—does that hold or not?

CRITO: Yes, it does.

SOCRATES: Then, following on what we have agreed, this has to be examined—whether it is right for me to try to get away

c from here without being released by the city, or whether it is not right. And if it seems right, then let us try; but, if it does not, we are to drop it. As for the considerations which you mention about the spending of money and about reputation and about the upbringing of children, I'm afraid those are really the notions of those many people who, without any understanding, would lightly kill a man and indeed bring him back to life again, if they were able to. But we, on the other hand, since the argument thus persuades us, should consider nothing else at all save what we just now mentioned, namely whether we shall be acting rightly in laying out money and giving thanks to those who will get me

d out of here—by 'we' I mean rescuers and rescued alike—or whether we shall really be acting wrongly in doing all those things. And, if it appears that we would be doing what was wrong, then surely we must not take into account as against doing wrong either our having to die if we stay here and do nothing, or our having to suffer anything else.

CRITO: I think that what you *say* is good, Socrates—but do look at what we are to *do*.

SOCRATES: Let us examine it together, good friend, and, if you

e have any counterargument to my argument, produce it and I shall do what you say. Otherwise, stop right now, dear man, saying the same thing over and over, that I must get away from here against the city's will; I attach much importance to acting in this matter having persuaded you, rather than against your will. Now consider the basic principle of our enquiry, to see if for

49 you it is satisfactorily stated, and try to reply to my questions in what you think to be the best way.

CRITO: I'll certainly try.

SOCRATES: Do we say that on no account are we to act unjustly

if we can help it? Or that in some cases one is to act unjustly, in
others not? Is it the case that there is no way in which doing
what is unjust is either good or honourable, as we have many
times agreed in the past? Or have all those things that we used to
agree on been discarded in these last few days? Have you and I
b   at our age, Crito, been all this time earnestly conversing with
each other and failing to notice that we are no different from
children? Or isn't it above all the case that things are as we used
to maintain before—that, whether the public says so or not, and
whether we have to bear a fate that is harder even than our
present, or whether we get an easier fate, acting unjustly is
utterly bad and shameful for the man who does it? Is that what
we say or not?

CRITO: It is what we say.

SOCRATES: In no circumstances then must one act unjustly.

CRITO: No, indeed.

SOCRATES: Then a man who has been unjustly treated must
not act unjustly in return, as most people think—for in *no* circumstances must one act unjustly.

CRITO: Apparently he should not.

c   SOCRATES: Well, what about this? Must one treat people
badly, Crito, or not?

CRITO: Certainly not, Socrates.

SOCRATES: Well. For a man who has been treated badly to give
back bad treatment in return—is that, as most people say, just,
or is it unjust?

CRITO: It is not just at all.

SOCRATES: For perhaps treating men badly does not differ at
all from treating them unjustly.

CRITO: That's true.

SOCRATES: Then one must neither return unjust treatment to
any men nor treat them badly, no matter what treatment one
d   gets from them. And look out, Crito, that in conceding these
points you do not agree to something which is in fact contrary to
your view; for I know that only a few people do or will hold this
view. So, between those who hold such a view and those who do
not there is no common ground of argument, but they necessarily
look down on each other when they see their respective stand-
points. Therefore, do you too consider very thoroughly whether
you share my view with me, and whether we are to make that the

L

starting point of our deliberations, namely that it is never the part of an upright man either to act unjustly or to return unjust treatment for unjust treatment received, or, if he is being badly treated, to defend himself by retaliating with bad treatment—

e   or whether you dissociate yourself from, and do not share, the principle from which I started. For I myself have believed this for a long time, and still do; but, if you have formed some other opinion, say so and instruct me. However, if you hold to our old view, then listen to the next point.

CRITO: But I do hold to it and agree with it: speak on.

SOCRATES: Well, here's the next point, or rather question. Must a man do whatever he has agreed to do, provided that what he has agreed to do is right, or is he to act deceitfully?

CRITO: He must do it.

SOCRATES: Now observe what follows. If we go away from here

50   without persuading the city to let us go, do we treat some badly, and those at that whom least of all we should treat badly—or not? Do we stand by our agreements (if they are right) or not?

CRITO: I have no answer to your question, Socrates; for I don't understand it.

SOCRATES: But look at it this way. Suppose, as we are about to run away from here (or whatever else it should be called) the laws and state of Athens were to confront us and say:

'Tell us, Socrates, what is it that you have in mind to do? Do

b   you intend to do anything else by this exploit to which you are putting your hand than to destroy both ourselves the laws and the entire city—at least as far as you can? Or do you think it is possible for that city to exist and not to be overthrown in which the decisions of courts do not prevail, but by the actions of individuals are set aside and made ineffective?'

What shall we say, Crito, in answer to those questions and others of that kind? For there is a lot that one could say, especially if one were a public speaker, in support of this law which was being destroyed, the one that declares that court decisions, once

c   reached, are binding. Or shall we say to them: 'Yes, that is what I intend, for the city wronged us and gave the wrong verdict at the trial'? Shall we say that—or what?

CRITO: Emphatically that, Socrates.

SOCRATES: Then what if the laws replied:

'Socrates, was that what was agreed between ourselves and

you, or was it that you would abide by the judgments of the city's courts?'

Then, if we showed suprise at their saying that, perhaps they would go on: 'Socrates, do not be surprised at what we say, but answer us—since it is your own practice to use question and
d   answer. Come now, what charge do you have against us and Athens that you are trying to destroy us? First, did we not beget you, and was it not through us that your father married your mother and produced you? Explain then, do you have some complaint against the marriage laws among us, that we are not as we should be?'

'I have no complaint,' I should say.

'Well, is it the laws concerning the upbringing of children, together with the education which you received? Or didn't the
e   laws ordained for that area prescribe well, when they ordered your father to provide you with a cultural and physical education?'

'They prescribed well,' I should say.

'Well. Now, since you were born, brought up and educated, could you deny, first, that you were our offspring and servant— both yourself and your forefathers? And, if that is so, then do you think that justice is on all fours for you and for us, and do you think that whatever we try to do to you it is just for you to do back to us? Or is it that, on the one hand, as regards justice you were not on equal terms with your father, or with your master (if you happened to have one), so as to give back to them what treatment you received from them—it would amount to your
51   not talking back when you were criticised, and not hitting back when you were struck, and not behaving in any other similar manner? But, on the other hand, in relation to your native land and its laws, will that be allowable to you, so that, if we try to destroy you, believing that to be just, then you too will attempt to the best of your ability to destroy in return us your laws and your country, and will you say that in doing that you are doing what is just, you the man who really cultivates virtue? Or are you so clever that it has escaped your notice that your country is more to be prized and revered, and is more sacred than your
b   mother, your father and all the rest of your forebears, and is held in greater esteem both among gods and among men (those who have understanding); and that you must pay honour to, and be

more submissive, even servile, to your country when it is angry than to your father; and that you must either persuade it or do what it commands, and that you must undergo without fuss anything it orders you to undergo, whether it is a beating or imprisonment, or whether it lead you out to war, to be wounded or to die; that that is what you have to do, and that is how justice is, and that you must not give ground or withdraw or leave your post, but in war and lawcourts alike, and everywhere else too you must do whatever your city and country orders, or else per-

c suade it in accordance with where justice really is; and that to use violence against either mother or father is impious, and that far less even than against them is it to be used against your country?'

What shall we reply to that, Crito? That what the laws are saying is true, or not?

CRITO: It seems true to me.

SOCRATES: 'Consider next, Socrates,' perhaps the laws would say, 'whether we are correct in asserting this, that you are not trying to treat us justly in what you are trying to do. For we,

d having begotten, nurtured and educated you, and having given to you, as to all the rest of the citizens, your share of all the fine things that we could, declare, by the fact of granting the privilege to any Athenian who wishes it, when he comes of age and sees how things are in the city, and sees us the laws, that anybody who is not satisfied with us is permitted to take what belongs to him and to emigrate to wherever he pleases. And not one of us laws stands in the way or forbids it if one of you wishes to go to a colony, in the event that we and Athens do not satisfy him, or if he wishes to go and remove himself elsewhere—we do not stop

e him going wherever he wishes, keeping what he owns. But whoever of you stays behind, seeing the way in which we decide our cases in court and the other ways in which we manage our city, we say that he has thereby, by his act of staying, agreed with us that he will do what we demand of him; and we say that the man who does not obey wrongs us in three ways: that he does not obey us his parents, that he does not obey us who brought him up, and that, having agreed to obey us, he neither does so nor persuades us, if there is anything which we are not doing right; although we propose rather than harshly demand

52 that he do what he is told to do, although we allow him one of two

choices, either to persuade us or to do as we say, he does neither. Now we say that you too, Socrates, will be subject to these charges, if you do what you have in mind; and in your case this applies not less than to other Athenians, but more than to almost anyone.'

Then, if I were to say, 'Now, why?', perhaps they would attack me quite justifiably by saying that, as a matter of fact, I have given this agreement to them more emphatically than almost any other Athenian. For they would say:

b   'Socrates, we have strong proof that you are satisfied with us and the state. For, if you were not more than usually satisfied, you would never have remained in residence here more than is usual for other Athenians: you never left the city for a festival, except on one occasion for the Isthmus, you never went any-where else except on military service, you never went abroad as other people do; nor did you have any desire to acquaint your-

c   self with another city or with other laws, but we and our city were enough for you. So strongly did you choose us and agree that you would fulfil the role of a citizen under us; apart from everything else you fathered children here, showing that the city pleased you. Then again, at the time of the actual trial you could, if you had wanted, have put forward banishment as the sentence which you thought would be appropriate, and what you are now trying to do against the city's will you could then have done with it. But you at that time prided yourself on not complaining if you had to die, you chose, so you said, death in preference to exile. Yet now you are neither ashamed of those

d   protestations, nor do you show regard for us the laws, as you try to destroy us; you are behaving just as the meanest kind of slave would, trying to run away contrary to the compacts and agree-ments by which you covenanted with us to conduct yourself as a citizen of Athens.

'First, then, give your answer to this question of ours, whether we are right in maintaining that you have, not by what you have said but by what you have done, agreed to live under us as a citizen? Or is that not the truth?'

What are we to reply to that, Crito? Can we do anything but agree with them?

CRITO: We have to agree, Socrates.

SOCRATES: 'Then are you doing anything else,' they would say, e 'but violating the compacts and agreements made with us, agreements which you entered into victimised neither by coercion nor by misrepresentation; nor were you forced to make up your mind in a hurry, but you had seventy years, in which it was possible for you to move away if we were not satisfactory to you, or if the agreements seemed to you to be unjust. But you chose neither Sparta nor Crete, which you assert on every occasion to

53 be states with good laws,[1] nor any other city in Greece or abroad —indeed you were away from the city less even than the lame, the blind and the rest of the physically handicapped. It is quite clear that you above all other Athenians were pleased with your city and with us, its laws—for who would be pleased with a city without laws? And now indeed do you stand by your agreements? You do, if you are persuaded by us, Socrates; and you will not become a figure of ridicule for leaving the city.

'For consider now, if you commit these transgressions and do something wrong in any of these ways, what good will you do

b either to yourself or to those close to you? As far as the latter are concerned, it is fairly clear that they will risk being prosecuted themselves and being deprived of their citizenship or their property. While, as for yourself, if you go to one of the nearby cities, to Thebes or to Megara—for they both have good systems of law—you will be arriving there, Socrates, as an enemy of the state, and everybody who cares for their cities will look at you with suspicion as a destroyer of laws, and you will reinforce the jury's opinion, so that they will be convinced that they gave the

c correct verdict; for anybody who is a destroyer of laws would certainly be believed to be a destroyer of youth and of witless men. Will you then avoid cities with good laws, and men of the most decent kind? And, if you do that, will life be worth living for you? Or will you try to associate with those men and be shameless enough to converse with them—what will you say to them, Socrates? Will it be what you say here, that virtue and justice are the most valuable things men have, together with the

d usages and institutions of law? And do you not think that "the

---

[1] It is interesting, if historically correct, that Socrates admired those two states for their legal systems. Plato in his final work, the *Laws*, written some forty or more years later, took the same pair of states as his starting point; from criticism of the defects of their legal systems he developed a legal code for his own Utopia.

Socrates business" will appear discreditable? You certainly should. Maybe you will keep away from these parts, and end up instead in Thessaly among Crito's friends. For there there is extreme disorder and lack of moral discipline; and perhaps they would take pleasure in hearing your funny story—how you escaped from prison by putting on some disguise, by wearing a jerkin or some other such outfit as runaways use, and altering your appearance. And will nobody remark that, as an old man
e   with very likely only a short time left to live, you had the presumption to want so much to hang on to life, while violating the most important laws? Perhaps not, if you do not trouble anybody; otherwise you will hear many remarks, Socrates, that will be unworthy of you. You will live by insinuating yourself into everybody's favour and behaving like a servant to them—what will you be doing but eating well in Thessaly, as though you had travelled there just for food and drink? As for that talk about
54   justice and the rest of virtue, where, tell us, will that be? But is it that you want to live for the sake of your sons, to bring them up and educate them? Will you do that by taking them to Thessaly, making foreigners of them, so that they can enjoy that too? Or, instead of that, will they be better brought up and educated if they are brought up here, with you still alive but not with them— for your friends will take care of them? Is it really the case that, if you go away to Thessaly, they will take care of them, but that, if you go away to the next world, they will not? Surely, if there
b   is anything to be got from those who call themselves your friends, you must suppose that they will help in that way.

'Now, Socrates, in obedience to us who reared you, do not make either children or life or anything else to be of more account that what is just, in order that when you reach the other world you may have all that to present in your defence before the rulers there. For, if you behave in the way you propose, it does not seem that it will be better for you here, or more just in relation to men or heaven, nor for any of your friends either; and
c   it will not be the better for you when you arrive there. But, as things now stand, you will leave here, if you do, wronged not by us the laws but by men; on the other hand, if you depart having so shamefully returned injustice for injustice and bad treatment for bad treatment, violating, that is, your own agreements and compacts made with us, and behaving badly towards those

whom least of all you should treat in such a way (we mean your-self, your friends, your country and ourselves), then we shall be angry with you while you live, and our brethren the laws in the other place will not receive you kindly there, knowing full well

d   that you have tried, for your part, to destroy us. Do not let Crito persuade you to follow his advice rather than ours.'

That, Crito my dear friend, be assured is what I believe I hear them saying, just as the celebrants of the Corybantic rites believe they hear the sound of the pipes; and the echo of their arguments reverberates in my mind, and makes me unable to hear anything else. But understand that, as to what I now believe, if you have anything to say against it, you will be wasting your time. Nevertheless, if you think you will achieve anything more, have your say.

CRITO: There is nothing, Socrates, that I can say.

e   SOCRATES: Well, let it be, Crito, and let us do things this way, since this is the way in which God is leading us.

Index locorum

General index

Agreement (*see also* Socratic arguments *and* Socratic principles), 43, 77–9; and 'as if' choice, 90–1; and compulsion, 88–90; and freedom, 93, 104, 106–8; and political activity, 97–100, 109; as continuous process, 93; hypothetical, 94–7; tacit and implied, 80–93, 99–104
Allen, R. E., 60
Anaximander, 54
Arginusae case, 50–2
Athens, laws of, 9, 31, 42, 53
attempt, criminal, 121–5, 129–30

'because it is the law', 72–3
Brandwood, L., 3
Burnet, John, 54

character, ethics of, 126, 132–3
children, *see* parents
communication, 101–4
consequences, and generalisation, 116–18
Consumer Credit Act, 78
contract, law of, 78
convention, 80, 85–6, 101–4
court orders, 8–9, 25, 38, 41–6, 56–8
cowardice, 11, 13–14, 16, 48
Criminal Law Act, 123n

democracy, 30, 49, 84
destruction, *see* Socratic arguments
Devlin, Patrick, 133–4
disobedience: and destruction, *see* Socratic arguments *and* Socratic principles; and disgrace, 47–9; civil, 27, 30–41, 52, 111
Dworkin, R., 31

education, 9–11
enemies, 8
experts (knowledgeable, reasonable men), 14, 17
expression, 80, 100–4

fairness, 25, 75, 82, 92, 118, 135–40
freedom, 93, 104; to emigrate, 81–2, 104–8
friendship, 6–7, 10

games, 42–3, 85–90, 92, 98

harm, 14, 21, 122–6; and injury, 19–20
Hart, H. L. A., 69
health, 17
Hume, David, 126

immigrants, 89–90
impiety, 41, 52, 58
intention, 122–6, 130, 132–3

James, Gene, 57
Jones, J. Walter, 53n
justice (*see also* fairness, Law, rightness *and* Socratic principles), 10, 18–22, 25–7, 56–8, 68, 70, 94, 96–7; and impiety, 52

Kant, Immanuel, 116
Kelsen, Hans, 42

Law (laws): and justice, 19, 41, 50–2, 54–61; and morals, 33–9, 53, 109, 130–2; and nature, 53–4; and statute, 53–4; as parents (*see also* Socratic arguments), 22, 63, 71; as persons, 28–9; enacted, 53; real and actual, 55, 60–1; unwritten, 53–4
Leon of Salamis, 52, 71
Locke, John, 81

Martin, Rex, 55
mens rea, 123, 125–6, 130
Model Penal Code, U.S., 123n
morals (*see also* Law *and* reasons), subjectivity of, 48
Murphy, J. G., 16

obey ($\pi\epsilon\acute{\iota}\theta\epsilon\sigma\theta\alpha\iota$), 45